BLIND PASSENGER

Dr. Melissa Tate

Blind Passenger
By Dr. Melissa Tate

Copyright @ 2015 by Dr. Melissa Tate

Published by
Meditate & Mingle DBA Dr. Melissa Tate

For permission requests, please direct all inquiries to:
BlindPassenger2015@gmail.com

For more information visit
www.DrMETate.com

Unless otherwise indicated all Scripture quotations are from the New King James and New Living Translations of the Holy Bible.

Edited by Katrina L. Lynch

Book Design by
www.DivineTouchMulitmedia.com
www.ProfitAndGrowthUnlimited.com

Images by
Aaron T. Atkinson

Artwork by
Anthony Scruse

Printed in the United States of America
ISBN: 0692549935
ISBN-13: 978-0692549933

Dear Blind Passenger,

I get it. I know how you feel and where you've been—not just because I've read about it or because I've counseled people through it, but because I've lived it. As you will read, I am truly transparent in sharing my personal journey through relationships that were heavily effected by drugs, alcohol, and emotional instability. I've come to recognize that my story is more universal than I initially realized. So, I'm breaking down some of my untold experiences to elicit necessary conversations about relationship dynamics, the impact of drugs and alcohol on the family, and the experience of managing mental instability amongst our loved ones.

This book is for those who see the "working single mother, very decisive, juggling it all, classy and professional Dr. Tate" of today with no idea of the shameful feelings I've had and the dark emotional spaces I've been. Many have asked how. They ask how I have been able to move forward without bitterness. How was I able to walk away from broken relationships? How do I have such a presence of calm and strength despite a history of being brokenhearted and betrayed by some of my closest loved ones?

First and foremost, it's by the grace and will of God that my image today does not indicate where I've been. Secondary to that, I decided a long time ago that I had no desire to be cloaked in bitterness, tears, and resentment. It wasn't who I was raised to be and it is not a reflection of who I aim to be. I just decided.

Did you forget that you have the power to decide who you are and what your story will be? Your present circumstance does not predict your future because you have decisions. I know it sounds very simplistic, but it is powerful in its own accord. It may be scary and sometimes emotional; but it is your decision that evokes change.

As a blind passenger in remission, this book offers both a personal and professional perspective of broken, emotionally unstable relationships. I will talk intimately about what allowed me to be decisive in my journey. I hope you receive it in a healing and sincere fashion. It is with nothing but validation and understanding that I offer my personal and professional thoughts to you.

Warmest Regards,

Dr. Melissa Tate

Table of Contents

$\mathscr{I}$ntroduction

We've all been there at some point. It was a friend, coworker, parent, sibling, boyfriend, or spouse who took you on their roller coaster ride of addiction, emotional tirades, alcoholism, or mental illness. Initially, things may have seemed okay. You make excuses for them by telling yourself; they're a good person or fun to be around. You've been able to pass off incidents as isolated, and you've given them the "benefit of the doubt". After all, a few thrills and bumps in the road are to be expected in any relationship, right? Over time, the dips and dives are so consistent that it becomes the new normal.

Mental illness and addiction do not discriminate, so being a clinician has not excused me from difficulties in my personal affairs. This book is a journey of self-disclosure and transparency, written as a juxtaposition of my personal and professional selves. I've written three personal, memoir-esque chapters of my personal experiences being a blind passenger. Through two broken marriages and a damaged sibling bond, I will illustrate the internal struggle I experienced being a passenger on the emotional and chemical rollercoaster of my loved ones. In my stories, their actual names have been replaced with a mythological caricature who possessed the qualities that led our relationships astray. You will see that I am fully transparent and raw in my depiction of these relationships. I've been in some dark, emotionally gritty spaces and have experienced some things for which I'm not proud of. Nevertheless, I'm able to own them for what they are and for what I've learned from them.

Each chapter of intimate self-disclosure and transparency paves the way for a Q&A style "necessary conversation" about my personal experience and pulls from my professional, therapeutic knowledge base of working through the topic at hand. After my share of soul searching, learning, praying, understanding, and making sense of my choices—(coupled with three degrees in psychology and ten years of professional mental health practice)—I've been able to merge my personal and professional experiences to facilitate therapeutic growth in the counseling of relationships. I am able to genuinely validate and help transform the lives of others as a result of experiencing and overcoming some of the darkest and most shameful moments of my life. In essence, I have been gifted an intuitive understanding of my blind passenger experience and relationship problems, in order to walk in my divine purpose of sharing it with you.

The closing section of this book provides therapeutic recommendations for restoring a sense of self amidst the emotional rollercoaster and discusses several ways to confront the blindness we have in our unhealthy relationships. This is difficult conversation, but necessary in all respects. In my practice, I have seen value in this discussion for both personal and generational family growth. In one way or another, we are all blind passengers. The emotions felt in proximity to a loved one's instability is real. Figuring out what or who is driving the emotional rollercoaster, is the gateway for you and your significant others to receive help.

Dr. Melissa E. Tate

Psychology Consultant and Licensed Professional
Charlotte, North Carolina

Conversation One

Thony

Thony

is a modern derivative of Phthonus,

the spirit of envy and jealousy. In Greek

mythology, he was associated in particular

with the jealous passions in matters of love

having killed each one of his wives due

to suspicions of adultery.

My thoughts seemed to hiccup from time to time. Barely one year into a labored marriage and I felt stupid that it was already in shambles. Truth be told, I knew from the beginning that it wouldn't last.

I met Thony (*pronounced Tony*), in 1997 during my senior year of undergrad. I was studying psychology at the University of Maryland in Baltimore County and I worked full-time as a commuting student. He was working multiple odd jobs here and there, bouncing at the nightclub where we met and working in the gardening department at Walmart; but his intelligence was quite apparent. Presently living in a shabby bachelor pad apartment in Baltimore City, he had previously studied law and business at an HBCU in Louisiana. He had stacks of books, magazines, and DVD's on the shelves which prompted endless conversation between us such topics as philosophy, religion, politics, pop culture, music, television, … you name it. He had a tendency to be somewhat opinionated, but I saw goodness in him and genuinely enjoyed his conversation and company. It wasn't long before we were together on a daily basis.

A few months into our dating, Thony accepted a great job offer in his home state of Georgia, which seemed to elicit his first proposal. There was no ring, but he was down on one knee as I sat on the edge of my bed, "Melissa I can't see my life without you." As sweet as it was, it seemed like things were moving too fast. I was pretty secure in my Maryland world as I was finishing my last year of coursework at UMBC. I remember the look of disappointment on his face as he stood up and left the house. However, it didn't stop us from spending nearly every day together He was very dedicated to me and always attentive. At one point in time, I wasn't feeling well. Under doctor's orders I had to change my diet and assume more rest, he was right there by my side trying to cheer me up. On a regular basis, he made a point to do things for me, like wash my car or bring me little surprises. Loyal and endearing, we enjoyed a lot of laughs together. I felt comforted by his presence.

The summer of 1998, we traveled to Georgia to visit his family — a loving, very welcoming, circle of people who reminded me of my own family. That sealed the deal in my eyes. I couldn't deny his second proposal. Thony and I were engaged just before my 22nd birthday. We had only been together for a little over a year, but I had grown to love him. He was my best friend and the thought of us being separated made me realize how much I would miss him.

Things were going well, but they were not always Georgia peachy. He was a little irritable at times, particularly in situations with other people. Whether we were driving up the street, walking through the mall, or out to eat at a restaurant, he was always perceptive to other men checking me out. In one situation, we were out for drinks and I saw a childhood friend. We had essentially grew up together because our parents bowled in the same weekly league. We ran around the bowling alley and arcade together for years. A mere unanticipated "heeeey" and wave across the bar prompted a firestorm of questions. Initially there was an eerie silence. There was minimal eye contact with me, but his eyes were lurking around the restaurant. I asked him what the matter was. He replied, "Nothing." Before long, he seemed to get all puffed up in his chest. With a deep accusing tone he said, "How do you know him? Have you dated him?" My explanation got the side eye and a cold shoulder, as if to say, "Yeah, Ok. Whatever". He took a deep breath and said, "Let's just go". His strides were gaping as we proceeded to the car. The tension was rising with each step. "It's disrespectful for you to wave at another man. You got me lookin' stupid!" His reaction made no sense to me. I found myself trying to defend it, but I didn't see that I had done anything wrong. There was absolutely nothing to explain, hide, or defend: yet there I was riding in the passenger seat explaining and defending myself until the thickness of silence set in.

The next day it was as if it never happened. No major discussion ensued, except maybe an "I love you" or an extra-long seemingly apologetic hug. I guess the "disrespect" he felt the night before, simply dissipated throughout the night. But it was bound to rise when another situation presented itself. It didn't take long. A month or so later, I invited some friends over to my parent's house for a summer cookout. Once again, he was aloof and withdrawn. Any group laughter or inside jokes shared between my friends were buzz-killed by his awkward lack of reciprocation. I kept a social smile while everyone was there. Later on I found out that he was fixed on my best friend's roommate, "It seems like he has a crush on you. He was looking at me funny." My denial had me labeled "naïve". Needless to say, meeting my friends didn't go so well. And in my eyes, there was no sense in arguing or explaining. So I swept it under the rug. *Note to self: Avoid social gatherings.*

Life went on as usual. Around the time of my winter graduation, I found out we were pregnant. Thony was settled into his job in Georgia and setting up residence for us. Nervously excited and already engaged, the news merely expedited the wedding plans. Married in February 1999, our first marital argument occurred on *Mr. and Mrs. Day One*. In the hotel after the wedding, I was up the hallway from our hotel suite talking with my new sister-n-laws, aunts, and family. I was sharing some leftover wedding cake with them and having a few laughs. Thony called their hotel room asking where I was, complaining that I had been there too long. When I left the room, he was in the company of his best man, so I was confused by his urgency and questioning. I was less than 100 yards away spending time with my new family. Jokingly, I smoothed things over in front of everyone telling them that they got me in trouble and soon left for our suite.

When I entered our bedroom Thony was sitting in the dark at the table. My attempts to lightheartedly explain were derailed when he threw a glass of Hennessey against the wall. Once the yelling match ensued, I told him he was being irrational, and that if this is how our marriage was going to be I wasn't going to stay with him. He called me childish, saying we were married now and that I couldn't leave. In his words, "You're my wife now". He was right. The permanence of my situation paralyzed me. I had a pit in my stomach, filled with uncertainty about my future, this marriage, and our growing family. But I was stuck. All of the signs of jealous possession from the previous year and a half of our dating and engagement were swirling in my head. How could I be so stupid? Apparently I was "naïve", but it was too late. I was 3 months pregnant and several hours into marriage. There was so much money, time, and planning put into this one day and I knew the prognosis for a long-term loving relationship was bleak. I felt trapped, but I saw no other recourse. I had to see it through.

Thirteen months later, there I stood in the foyer of our Georgia home, drifting off into a daze. *Hiccup.* I had become accustomed to getting stuck in my own thoughts since sharing them with my husband didn't seem to be of any use. The front door slammed behind him and he drove away in my car. My mind was swirling with confusion, shame, anger, and helplessness. The list goes beyond my articulation. Imani began to rustle in her crib. Her whimpers pulled me back to the reality of my life. I walked upstairs into her bedroom to lift her from her restlessness. As I held her to my chest, bouncing her back to sleep, I remember thinking that I couldn't do it anymore.

I returned downstairs to use the house phone and I made two calls. "Kelly, are you busy?"

Kelly was married to Thony's cousin. They lived a few miles away on the other side of the train tracks. We often got together to entertain the kids: her two boys and my baby girl. It broke up the monotony of the day. Having moved away from my family in Maryland to be with him, I didn't have much to call my own. She was the closest thing I had to a legitimate friend while living there that year. As two stay-at-home moms, I spent more time with her than anyone.

"Well, I'm about to …"

I don't fully recall what she said. Whatever it was, she must have heard something different in my voice that day. As much as our bond had grown through the play dates and mommy talks, I'd never told her that I felt trapped in my marriage. I never told her that I was embarrassed for choosing such a broken, emotionally unstable spirit of a man as my husband. I never told her that my spirit was breaking in the process. And apparently that day, I didn't have to tell her much at all. She stopped short in her list of things to do, saying, "I'm on my way." I believe it was unspoken and that it went without saying that I needed her in that moment. I believe she anticipated that this very phone call would occur.

As I hung up the phone, a frenzy set in. I was halfway relieved that she answered my call, yet filled with mixed anxiety about what would happen next. I was moments away from breaking through the clouds of confusion that plagued me from the very beginning of this marriage, but I was instantly fueled with worry. Thony was sometimes irrational in his thoughts, very defensive, and he always wanted his way. He didn't take kindly to rejection or criticism, and he was unwavering when he had his mind made up about anything. If he returned to the house while I was walking out the door with our six-month old daughter and a bag of clothes for the two of us, it wasn't going to be pretty.

"911, what's your emergency?"

I asked for an officer to come to my house in case my husband returned in the middle of my packing. In retrospect, I'm amazed at my focus. Even though I had more than enough reason to call the police before, it never crossed my mind once. It didn't take long for the officer to arrive. I explained what was happening and that my cousin was in route. "If my husband comes back too soon, things will get real ugly, real fast." My heart was racing along with my thoughts. I stood there, bouncing Imani in my arms looking upstairs thinking about the things I needed to pack. My thoughts hiccupped once again...

Several Months Earlier – 3AM

Thony awakened me, smelling of alcohol. He didn't drink too often, but had been out with his friend that evening. It was the night of the baby shower, so they were celebrating.

"Miss...wake up. We need to talk," he said with a gruff tone of voice. This was a pretty signature tone coming from him, particularly when he was ready to have an intense conversation. His voice was a deep baritone. It was as if he was scolding me already. I had been lying down for hours. I wasn't asleep. How could I sleep in the aftermath of yet another ridiculous tirade, which ended in him kicking my parents out of the house?

My parents surprised me by visiting from Maryland to be present for the baby shower and the birth of their first grandchild. Thony decided on day two of their visit that he was not in the mood for houseguests. With very little discussion or a hint of where this was coming from, he politely and abruptly asked them to leave. Just the night before, the four of us were playing Scrabble at the kitchen table. It was light-hearted and fun. For the first time in months, I was fully content. But I guess that's all he could stand. He had just returned to the house after an early morning job interview, which evidently didn't go well, so he was done being hospitable. He wanted them to leave and he didn't have a problem with telling them. My parents responded with brief retort.

I'm sure they had more than a mouthful to say, but they bit their tongues and gathered their belongings with little debate. By the end of the hour, they were leaving the house in their own cloud of confusion, worry, sadness, and anger. Thony's parents took them in for a stay. They were embarrassed by his behavior and wanted to accommodate the situation the best they could.

I was mortified. It was just hours away from the baby shower, where I was to be the center of attention. Yet, my child's father made my skin crawl. He bought me flowers and a big Tigger stuffed animal just as the house began to fill with shower-goers. I guess, that was supposed to smooth things over. I wore an obligatory smile on the outside, but I was ashamed on the inside. So, sleep didn't come easy for me that evening.

Nine months pregnant, I barely sat myself up before he started ranting, "Your mother is a bitch! That bitch..." I threw my legs to the side of the bed and stood up to leave the room. I wasn't going to sit there and listen to whatever justification he thought he had to cast blame on my parents for their surprise visit. He pled with me to stay and talk, grabbing at me repeatedly. I snatched my arms away and tried to walk around him through our moonlit bedroom. Hands on hands, yelling and snatching, and more hands. It all happened so fast. As I approached the bedroom door, BANG! My forehead hit the wall and I slid to the floor, taking the same position as my unborn child.

I curled onto my hands and knees to protect my stomach and the baby girl growing inside of me who was feeling every moment of my stress. My stress equaled her stress. Still yelling and pleading for me to listen to him "because we're married now. He said to me, "We have to work this out. You can't just walk away." I just wanted him to leave me alone. I wanted him to stop touching me. I wanted him to stop yelling. As he turned on the bedroom light, I saw my blood had smudged the sky blue paint of the wall.

A combination of blood and tears dripped down my face. Thony continued to grab at me as I picked myself up off the floor and walked out of the bedroom, downstairs to the telephone. He continued to plead with me as I called his parents.

They answered the phone in a stupor. I must have sounded like a mad woman.

"Ma'am, why do you keep looking upstairs? Do you mind if I check around your house?"

Snapped back into reality by the officer designated to be my watchman, I put the baby in her car seat on the foyer floor as I gathered some of our belongings. The officer briefly walked around the house and then stood at the front door while I packed: diaper bag, duffle bag, and baby. That's all I needed to secure my next moves as Kelly pulled in the driveway. I didn't care about toys, furniture, or any of our material things. I just wanted to go. We pulled away from the yellow house with plantation shutters, a two-car garage, and silk, weathered flowers on each windowsill.

Kelly was inquisitive. "Who called the police? Are you okay? What's going on?" On the way to her house, I told her that I couldn't do it anymore.

Although this was certainly an urgent and unplanned situation, I don't think it took her by surprise. Everyone in the family was fully aware of the ups and downs of his personality. At times he was super sweet, fun loving, and quite witty. I remember staying up to the wee hours of the morning playing video games with him. Having lost his job, we'd binge for days on Play Station, order wings from the food truck on the corner, and laugh incessantly. We liked the same music, sometimes laying together in the quiet of the day listening to each other talk. Preparing for Imani's arrival brought some excitement. I hoped her presence would settle the insecurities I noticed. But fatherhood seemed to stir a mixture of other things within him. I had no idea that her infantile presence would be a threat.

"You love the baby more than me," he complained one morning as I breastfed her and rocked her to sleep. It sounded like the type of temper tantrum you hear from a jealous sibling. The sun had barely risen. I was sleep deprived and riddled with annoyance at the sight of a grown man's envy of his own child. I just sat there on the edge of the bed and stared off into space. I didn't have the words to respond, so he left the room in a huff.

She was in the way. A product of adoption, Imani was the only biological relative he knew. He was enamored with her resemblance to himself. But in his eyes, the bond I was forming with my baby girl was a problem. It kept him from feeling close to me, and it didn't seem to compare to the bond he wanted with her. At one-month old, he wanted me to leave Imani with his parents to go away with him on a trip. He didn't understand my refusal and decided to label it as Post-Partum Depression. I was depressed, but not because of the baby. I felt trapped.

Journal Entry - September 24, 1999

I am scared of this change, even though I know it's the best thing at this time. I physically have to get away. I can no longer take the daily mental voyages. I am misunderstood and repeatedly taken for granted. I am sad. I cannot express how I feel to my husband. It hurts to feel all alone in my marriage. I am losing myself. I am mentally exhausted and emotionally detached from him. I need to go. I need to clear my head.

I left for Maryland to spend time with my family and Imani was in tow. My mother connected me with a good family friend and counselor to talk about my marital struggles. I had a sense of comfort and peace when I was in Maryland. I felt like myself for the most part – no fake smiles, no eggshells to walk on, and no mood swings. I didn't want to go back. Thony pled and damn near demanded, "You need to come back here and work this out for our family." I hated the sound of his voice. And although I felt childish for shying away from the commitment I made before God, friends, and family, I dreaded the thought of returning to a house that didn't feel like home. After a week or two in Maryland, I begrudgingly returned.

We went to marital counseling. I can't say things got better, but they didn't get much worse. When Imani began to drink rice cereal from a bottle, he liked feeding her. He was very gentle and sweet, holding her in his lap while he played video games or watched TV. By four or five months, he laughed when she banged on her toys and tried to grab the remote control. She was growing beautifully – a very alert and happy baby. I often worried how the stress of the marriage affected her while she was inside my belly, but she didn't seem to miss a beat.

Thony's domineering personality continued to rear its ugly head from time to time. He didn't make a habit of putting his hands on me, but I was consistently on the receiving end of his mood swings. He wanted what he wanted, and he had a grand attitude and headstrong way of expressing himself. Whether at work or with family, he had a consistent sense of entitlement, for which he was aggressive. "Greed is good," he would say emulating Michael Douglas in *Wall Street*. This mantra resonated with him and fortified his ideas of success, power, and money. Being from a family of very high achieving professionals, he was very impassioned for greatness, but it didn't seem to manifest. At times, he seemed delusional with grandeur. It was hard to watch my handsome, intelligent, brawn, and articulate husband act in such a bizarre way. He would say I wasn't supportive. All I knew is that it didn't feel good to be unified in marriage with that type of narcissism. It wasn't me. My sister-in-law gave me a book by Stormie Omartian, *The Power of a Praying Wife*. I prayed to God for guidance and clarity. At that point in my life, I was the most prayerful I had ever been. Too blinded by shame to share my innermost thoughts with anybody, God was the only one to hear my honest and true voice.

After pulling away from the house, Kelly said she felt something was wrong on the other end of the phone, but she couldn't quite put her finger on it. Although she had never seen or heard of any dysfunction or tension between Thony and me, she knew I needed her in that moment. Once I opened up to her about some of the sordid details, she took me to her house. It wouldn't be long before he looked for me at Kelly's, so she arranged for me to stay the night at her friend, Melanie's, house. I called my parents and told my in-laws where I was. They all played a role in my exit plan, keeping my whereabouts secret when Thony called frantically wondering if they had talked to me. I was able to make arrangements for a one-way ticket home.

My parents were ready to receive me and their grandbaby, Miss Imani, with open arms. It was clear. I was leaving the house in which I'd been living and going home to. That house never really felt like home.

At Melanie's for the evening, the clouds became thinner and thinner. She showed me to a guest room with a daily calendar on the nightstand. The day's declaration: *"Arise and go thy way; thy faith hath made thee whole."* - Luke 17:19.

Imani means "faith" in Swahili – a name I chose for my child while she was growing inside of me. In my mind, the clarity I had been praying for was fortified with that subliminal message from God—and the creator of spiritual day calendars. Apparently they had been conspiring with Melanie to strategically place that message on the nightstand for me. I smiled to myself, humbly bowed my head, and whispered, "Thank you God.

Message received." This marriage stifled me for a spell, but I had all I needed to find myself again: my faith, my child, and my family – in that order.

Thony's aunt drove me to the airport the following day. I had a one-way ticket with no intention to return. He made attempts to rekindle things asking me to come back to Georgia, but I was pretty decided. After a few months, he came to Maryland for Imani's first birthday party. It was a little awkward being around him again, but I was willing to have him there as Imani's father — not my husband.

A few weeks later, we received a letter in the mail. In the envelope was a tri-folded, hand-written letter from Thony addressed *"To Imani and Mommy; Love Daddy"*.

It read:

"Dear Imani,

*How are you? Your mommy
tells me that you are learning and
attempting to pronounce new words
every day. She has also told me that
you are walking everywhere. Daddy
is so sorry for not being a part of
your daily growth during these
impressionable months. Please
forgive me. I was very mean to your
mommy and I forced her to leave. It
was inevitable that you would have
to leave with [her]. I miss you very
much. I miss your mommy
also...Everyday I regret hurting your
mommy and I regret being without
you. I missed your first steps and
your first words. These are
cherished events that no parent
should miss. I wish you were here*

so I could teach you how to read,
how to analyze, and how to
comprehend your new environment.
I will not be an absent father.

Imani, a piece of me dies each
day you and your mommy are apart
from me. I never realized how much
I loved and cherished you and your
mommy until you were gone. I can't
hold you, talk to you, see your smile,
caress you, soothe your pain, wipe
your tears, bathe you, change your
diapers, feed you, read to you, teach
you to walk, talk, brush your hair,
rock you to sleep, dress you, kiss
you, bond with you or see your ever
changing facial expressions. I am
very lonely and very, very sad.
When your cousins have piano

recitals, plays, and birthday parties,
I never attend. It is too painful for
me to witness their growth and
development and the love, praise,
and adulation their parents give
them. Knowing that I am not a
constant and daily presence in your
life is destroying me emotionally.

It is my destiny to share the
fruits of my resurrection with you
and your mommy. Through prayer
and understanding your mother and
I will redefine our love for each
other. Our relationship can be
strong and it can provide strength
and stability for you. With the
power of God and the love of two
parents, your future will be filled

44

with infinite possibilities and you
will be filled with limitless potential.

Love Forever,

Daddy"

We have not seen him since that birthday party and this is the last personal message he has written to either of us.

$\mathcal{N}$ecessary $\mathcal{C}$onversation #1

It's pretty apparent, Thony's family was quite willing to help you leave. Did that manifest any earlier?

His family is wonderful. I am blessed to have their unconditional love and support to this day. They often articulated a sense of responsibility to Imani and myself. His parents wanted to support me as if I were their own child. At the time, they were not fully aware of the magnitude of our difficulties. For those who knew some of the details our marriage, I believe they were in a catch-22 position, wanting to tread lightly with directing me to leave him and merely waiting for me to come to my own decisions in the matter. As the issues in the marriage began to unfold, they certainly acknowledged that there had been some pre-existing instability with him prior to our marriage.

Had you not been pregnant at the time, do you think you would have stayed after the incident?

This is hard to answer in hindsight, but my quick answer is no. I remember being hopeful that the presence of the baby would change his attitude and demeanor. I've come to recognize this as a common problem in relationships, *thinking your spouse will change when* _____. In essence, you wind up waiting to see if the *idea* of the relationship you have in your head will show up in living color. For me, I think I primarily stayed in the relationship to cultivate the idea of family. It won't be the last time that you hear of someone staying in a relationship for the children.

Why do you think Thony was never physically assaultive toward you again?

This is a great question. I honestly do not believe it was in his nature to be a physically aggressive person. He did not have a rowdy upbringing, nor was he raised in a culture of aggression, conflict, or crime. So in my mind, I think the combination of feeling overwhelmed with rejection and perhaps fears of abandonment, as well as a few drinks he had that evening, contributed to that incident of domestic violence.

Furthermore, there is research to support the association between acute heavy alcohol consumption and the occurrence of intimate partner violence (Leonard & Eiden, 2007). There is also a distinction between various types of domestic violence, in which my circumstance seems to have been *Separation-Instigated*

Violence. This is characterized as an unexpected act of violence typically triggered by the experience of traumatic separation and/or humiliation of some kind, in contrast to a long-term coercive and controlling form of violence (Kelly & Johnston, 2008). Having experienced his rage upon separation in the past, I was forced to be pretty aware of his response when I actually decided to leave the home with our daughter.

As a counselor, have you ever provided counseling for the aggressor?

Yes, I have counseled clients, both men and women, who enter counseling as the aggressor in domestic violence dispute. I'm able to work with them from an anger management perspective in identifying and communicating the emotions that lie beneath the rage. Men in particular are taught to "*man up*" and bottle their emotions; only to lash out when a trigger button is pressed. So often times, the anger comes from unspoken, unbridled fear, anxiety, embarrassment, worry or sadness that they are unable to identify or express accordingly. The more vulnerable emotions are bypassed, ignored, and masked by the more "*gender appropriate*" and power asserting response of anger. Breaking that emotional process down and allowing one the opportunity to confront and communicate accordingly from the ignored emotions, tempers the anger response. It is a powerful transformation to be a part of.

Do you recommend women maintain their own bank accounts as a protective measure if things turn bad?

Money and finances are certainly some of the foremost reasons that people remain in unhealthy relationships. As the primary breadwinner, men sometimes feel like its *"cheaper to keep her"* and they do not want to divide their earnings. For women, there's a feeling of uncertainty about how they will survive without the husband's income and financial support — particularly when there are children involved. Furthermore, economic abuse (i.e. withholding money, threatening to stop payment on bills, isolating one from the bank account) is another form of control that is used in abusive relationships.

In my personal situation with Thony, having resources by the way of loved ones, was the biggest catalyst in allowing me to make moves with some degree of comfort. I was not employed when I was married to Thony and I was financially dependent on him. I had my own credit card for emergencies, but I did not have an income at the time. His parents funded the plane tickets for Imani and I to return to Maryland. They have continued to provide child support, as well as emotional encouragement, for their granddaughter over the years.

So to answer the question more directly, —"Yes, having your own finances and resources likely strengthens the ability to make a decision." My biggest safety net was family and loved ones. Ultimately, I always had someplace to retreat to without judgment; but I had to fight through my "*blindness*" in order to use the support that was always there for me. People often want to keep up the façade that everything at home is going well and are sometimes embarrassed, ashamed, or feel burdensome when reaching out to others. I suggest you find a short-term support team somewhere; a

> *"Don't think of it as what you will lose, rather what you will gain."*

coworker, a friend, a therapist, a domestic violence shelter, a hotel, etc.—and fortify a long-term plan from there. Don't think of it as what you will lose, rather what you will gain. I left for safety and peace of mind, which is far more valuable than anything my husband had to offer.

As a sports fan, I'm wondering how you feel about the domestic violence situations that have been prevalent with the NFL?

First of all, I'm glad the NFL is using these unfortunate situations to shed light on domestic violence and to bolster their policies on player conduct. There were definitely some inconsistencies in how cases were being handled amongst each team around the league. So it seems progress has been made on the media coverage of these violent situations. It's sad to see some of our nation's best athletes struggle in their personal lives. With their notoriety, it's easy to see them as "superhuman" and assume they don't have these issues; but to some degree it may actually be magnified because they are in the *limelight* where there is a tendency to overlook or excuse the behavior.

Specifically speaking, I was heartbroken watching the elevator assault between Ray and Janay Rice. Fortunately, but unfortunately, I think the video footage really brought people up close and personal with domestic violence in order to make the conversations happen. It was quite difficult to watch. But it was even more difficult to see how the family was vilified in the media and amongst public opinion. I'm face to face with human error and the fight for personal progress every day in my private practice, so perhaps I have a skewed perspective. But I just see them as people —*with flaws going through things like the rest of us*.

From a personal standpoint, I can identify with Janay's difficulty accepting the "victim" label. A victim is defined as a person harmed, injured, or killed as a result of a crime, accident, or other event or action. By definition, we are both victims. However, I tend to make a distinction between the definition and my mentality, which does not identify with a victim state. Some people prefer to be called a "survivor" or a "thriver" versus a victim because it is empowering. For myself, identifying as a victim is an awkward juxtaposition to my *"tomboy"* mentality because — it doesn't quite line up in my mindset. Nonetheless, I have a sense of compassion for all families involved in domestic dispute, both as having been a victim and as a therapist.

Conversation Two

Janus

Janus

is the ancient Roman God of

beginnings, transitions, gates, doors, endings,

and time. Commonly depicted with two faces—

one regarding what is behind and the other

looking toward what lies ahead—Janus

symbolizes the duality between two

opposing phases of transition, such

as progression from primitive to civilized.

I'm a happy social drinker. I drink, I dance, I laugh, and I get home safely, and it's all in the name of fun! I'm from a family of happy social drinkers. Our barbeques, birthday celebrations, cookouts, weddings, and even funerals have been known to have a drink or two (*or three*) involved. We gather, cook lots of food, play music, pull out a few decks of cards for poker or spades, and maybe play a few party games like Taboo or Pictionary. And at the end of the day, there was enough laughter to keep us on a high for days. It was the family camaraderie I've come to cherish.

In 2004, I became closely acquainted with a *not-so-happy* social drinker. As a native of the upper mid-west, Janus loved his beer and often quipped that he "drank more than the average man." We met at my first real job post-Master's, working on a Mobile Crisis Team in Baltimore City. We were two mental health therapists with similar interests and temperaments. We spent every day working with other therapists, nurses, and direct support staff serving the homeless, under-insured, drug addicted, and chronic mentally ill adults in the urban area. Despite working in close quarters with very little privacy, the staff seemed to function as a family in this fast-paced environment. Imagine *Grey's Anatomy* for urgent mental healthcare. We knew each other's ups and downs, weaknesses, strengths, and personal situations. Janus and I seemed to hit it off pretty well and became an item within my first few months on the job. We were two of a kind, – respected amongst our superiors and colleagues, and performed well at our job.

Before long Janus moved in with me at my parents' house, and we looked for a home of our own. We were engaged in July 2005. By then, he'd been around my family regularly, including my 6-year-old daughter. Janus and I were on the same page in regards to the type of relationship we wanted and our ideas about raising kids. He was very encouraging of my continued education and was always a gentleman. He swept me off my feet – by buying flowers, walking me to my car, making me a plate of food, rubbing my feet, and buying cute outfits. He even liked to cook! We watched a lot of movies and enjoyed the same type of TV shows; so from a daily lifestyle perspective, things felt seamless, except when he was drinking. He had grown quite comfortable at a local bar near the house, grabbing a few drinks 3-4 times each week. I'd never seen him ill with a hangover and he always got up for work the next day with the same professional, fun-loving attitude as the day before. So, I was naïve and didn't recognize his drinking as an issue. A sloppy night here and there was swept under the rug because I could see the man who loved to make me smile the next day. But eventually those drinking binges caught up to both of us.

The fun family gatherings that I grew up enjoying became a source of stress. Janus' one beer too many made him careless, loud-mouthed, and rude. When he'd slam money and chips on the table during poker, slur his words, and get "off his square," it changed the whole atmosphere in the room. I'd get the quiet side-eye from different family members, while Janus stumbled over his words and complained that someone was cheating him out of his money.

One New Year's Eve while playing cards with my parents and brother, literally felt like a scene from a Tyler Perry movie. After being told repeatedly to stop banging on the table, I yelled at him to "calm down." He felt disrespected and wandered out of the house. As the designated driver, I ended the night early to relieve us from further embarrassment, but the tirade was just beginning.

Speeding towards our house, with two children in the backseat, *my daughter and her cousin,* I blasted the radio to drown out the arguing. It was unreasonably loud. He was ranting about me making a scene. *"Really? I made a scene?"* I just wanted him to shut up.

Once home, I took the children in and led them to the bedroom. When I came out and sat on the couch, he stood over me saying...

"You disrespectful **bitch**! You **whore**!"

Without forethought, I smacked him across his face and stood in front of him. He kept his head turned in the direction of the slap.

"Ain't this 'bout a bitch," he said. "Oh, you like to put your hands on people."

I was instantly riddled with guilt, but more than anything, I was in defense mode. I stood face to face with him and I made myself very clear.

"Don't you EVER, in your LIFE, talk to me like that!"

He was so caught off guard that it seemed to break the tension immediately. He walked outside to smoke a Black & Mild, mumbling under his breath with each step.

I wondered how the night took such a downward spiral. What started as family fun got more uncomfortable with each beer. Watching his transformation from giddy excitement to an anxious level of sloppy arrogance was like watching Dr. Jekyll and Mr. Hyde. Sober Janus was my best friend– ever supportive, level-headed, and charming. Drunken Janus had a chip on his shoulder and seemed to take the slightest things personal. He wanted to have long, drawn out conversations about things that seemed unfair throughout his life: – stressors at work, his parents' divorce, and other things that happened in his family. Everything was fair game when there was beer to drink, and if he could help it, there was always beer to drink.

After I slapped him, he stayed outside a while, long enough for me to let my mind settle and fall asleep. In the middle of the early morning, I woke up next to him in a puddle of piss.

My fiancée couldn't hold his liquor through the night. He peed all over what was supposed to be our marital bed. I was disgusted to say the least. Given his drunken stupor, he didn't hear a word I said, but it didn't stop me from making an example of his foolishness. I lit into him with every ounce of my frustration. It wasn't the finest hour for neither of us. I honestly believed we'd hit rock bottom.

Janus and I were both remorseful about our actions. He made light of needing a diaper at night and seemed embarrassed about it all. I shared my concerns about the drinking binges, to which he didn't even try to defend himself. He made a concentrated decision to conduct himself differently and I was apologetic for slapping him. I had to face the jury on that one. My daughter, Imani, heard the arguing and a smacking sound. I couldn't tell her the truth. I explained it away.

Things settled in the house for some time. He drank less frequently and pretty much stayed home if he was going to drink. This allowed for two things: (1) no awkward family gatherings and

(2) he was usually asleep by the time I got home. So under those circumstances, there were no arguments or drunken tirades. I turned a blind eye to the drinking because he seemed to be keeping things in line. But it was just a matter of time before the restlessness set in and he ended up at the local bar.

One night at the onset of Spring 2006, Janus was stopped by an officer while driving home. He was charged with his first DUI. A second DUI came in less than 30 days. So, the man who prided himself on having no arrests or criminal offenses now had to deal with "real-world" consequences for his drinking. Needless to say, he faced jail time.

Initially, he was in such denial about his drinking issues. In general, he wanted to blame the police officer, the court system, and the *drinking and driving* laws.

"Drinking is legal. I can drink if I want. I'm not breaking any laws," he commented.

He had such an arrogance and air of entitlement when he was drunk, but he couldn't hold that attitude for long. Eventually, he had to face the truth. And without that truth, our pending marriage was in jeopardy.

Janus was mandated to court-monitored probation before judgment including: individual and group counseling, weekly AA meetings, a suspended driver's license, and random urine screens for a year. He had to get sober quickly. He didn't want to go to jail, so he followed through with his legal obligations. For the first time to my knowledge, he reluctantly said, "I'm an alcoholic." Once this acknowledgement spilled from his lips, I supported him.

He substituted alcohol for various energy drinks. I was extremely proud of him. Life moved on without a hitch. So much so, we were married in July of 2006 and our daughter, Erin, was born in December. Janus secured a new job after leaving the Mobile Crisis Team, so we talked a lot about his new management responsibilities. He was a little anxious about the role, but once again he seemed to be very well respected at work. For fun, we watched movies and went on family outings. For the first time since the beginning of our relationship, Janus was consistently doting and emotionally available as a husband and father. His mother visited from Milwaukee and marveled at how pleasant he was. I slept worry free. I no longer wondered whether he would get in an accident, be arrested, or pass out somewhere. He was home and he seemed to be at peace.

That is, until he received notice that his probation was clear. Approximately one year after the initial DUI and several months of sobriety,

Janus received a letter clearing him of his legal obligations. The next day, he celebrated with a beer…and the next day…and the next day. My husband reverted back to the drunken stranger I loathed. And with a new job, I was no longer privileged to see the sober, professional Janus that I worked with and ultimately fell in love with. Sober Janus put my mind at ease and reminded me that things were normal. But, when I got home from an evening class or a long day's work, all I saw was Drunken Janus. Sometimes I wasn't sure what I would come home to. But on more than one occasion, *Drunken Janus* was passed out on the couch while the kids greeted me at the front door at 9:30PM on a school night. He'd say, "Everybody's safe. There's no problem. They ate and they've had baths." My heart sank with each passing day. I was disappointed and ridiculously resentful because it felt like he'd given up on our family. I long joked that he'd been cheating on me with beer, and it was clear his mistress was back in town. Unfortunately, I knew this was the beginning of the end.

Our relationship took a sharp left turn after he resumed drinking. I reminded him what we had at stake. He minimized it. "I won't drink and drive," he said, as if that was a solution to his drunken belligerence and meager partnership. I felt like I was in a twilight zone. I was angry, irritable, and I didn't trust him to be my partner nor lead our family.

We were now the parents of two daughters; my oldest was 10 years old. She began to recognize the drinking pattern and in her naiveté talked about it quite freely when the situation allowed. This was not the example of a father I wanted for my children. Once again, I had to face the jury.

Why is daddy walking like that? Why is daddy talking like that? Daddy's having a sleepy day after going in and out all night.

I wanted to shush her, and had even contemplated telling her about how to keep "family business" inside of our home. In essence, I was about to blind my child to the reality of his drinking, but her eyes were open. I couldn't explain it away if I wanted to. And truth be told, I didn't want to. I'd rather remove my children from the likelihood of additional alcohol-laced arguments, then to live covering up a lie. I was tired. I was tired of making excuses for him and holding onto his dirty little secrets. I wanted it to stop. Her eyes opened my eyes.

Any alcoholic beverages brought into the house were poured out. I made it very clear where I stood on the matter. With each drink, he was killing our family and himself. His solution was to drink outside the home and stumble in at some ridiculous hour of the night while we all slept. One night in November 2007, right before Thanksgiving, brought that option to an end our union.

Erin, 10 months old at the time, woke up in her crib. Upon getting up to rock her back to sleep, I saw Janus standing at her crib with his eyes closed using it for a urinal. He was peeing on our daughter. I mashed his face with my open hand and screamed, "*What the hell are you doing?*" He barely knew what was happening.

"There you go putting your hands on people again; what's your problem," he said.

I was in shock. There I was in the middle of the night, bathing and changing our daughter because she was soaked with beer-tainted urine. I didn't sign up for that. Or did I? I never thought a few drunken nights in the honeymoon phase of our relationship would end up like this. I was blinded by love. I was blind to the lifestyle of a functional alcoholic. I was blinded by the good heart of "Sober Janus". I didn't want to believe that *Drunken Janus* was winning the battle inside of him, and I didn't want to believe alcohol was more important than our family.

I never emotionally recovered from that night in November. My husband wasn't apologetic or embarrassed. *Sober Janus* didn't want to talk about the incident and tried to act like it never happened. *Drunken Janus* was just as entitled and defensive as ever.

"So what? I can pee wherever I want," he said.

From that point, I emotionally divorced my husband. The papers weren't actually signed until the following spring, but my marriage was over.

My eyes were forever vigilant and my heart was on guard, trying to prepare for the next inevitable drunken night. I tried to go through the motions, but I was annoyed with the thought of having to pretend each day. I just couldn't recover from that incident regardless of what changes he said he would make. I dreaded going home at the end of the day. A fatigue came over me as I approached the house, and the soundtrack of my state of mind was Beyoncé's *Resentment* from the B-Day album.

> *Loving you was easy once upon a time*
> *But now my suspicions of you have*
> *multiplied*
> *And it's all because you lied.*
> *I only give you a hard time*
> *'Cause I can't go on and pretend like*
> *I haven't tried to forget this*
> *Because I'm much too full of resentment.*
> *Just can't seem to get over the way you*
> *hurt me*

Don't know how you gave another who
didn't mean a thing
The very thing you gave to me
I thought I could forgive you and I know
you've changed
As much as I want to trust you, I know it
ain't the same

I listened to it repeatedly, almost daily. The mistress Beyoncé sang about seemed to be a little different than mine, but the feelings were identical.

Janus, sensing my distance, eventually came to me saying, "I can't promise you I'll never drink again." Without hesitation I responded, "I can't promise you I'll stay in this marriage." I asked him to leave but he refused, saying he had no place else to go. The following morning, I packed some things for my daughters and myself. We moved out to stay with my parents. I was determined not to live a resentful life with an overwhelming expectation for my husband's sobriety, especially if he didn't have an equal expectation for himself.

Necessary Conversation #2

As a licensed professional, do you feel that you should have seen the signs earlier when it came to your exes?

I married my first husband when I was 22 years old. I didn't become a licensed mental health professional until I was 28 years old. My insight and experience with identifying mood and emotional instability and alcoholism was still maturing, as was I. Most readers have noticed a cleaner "*rebound*" from the second marriage as opposed to the first; which I contribute to maturity, experience, and having more of a clinical insight for what was happening. But, there's an interesting point to make in this question: *"The emotional investment I put forth in my personal life is different than the investment I have toward my clients in my professional life."* I have professional boundaries and limits to protect me at work. I'm able to practice empathy or compassion for those I work with in the office without clouding my judgment. And while at work, it's not my story, my emotions, or my family. So there are some safeguards in place that allow my opinions to remain objective. However, in my personal life, the boundaries are skewed. My emotions are involved. My guard is lowered. My empathy feels more like sympathy because I'm *IN* the process with them and I have an emotional investment in the outcome. You've often heard the phrase, *"Its business, not personal"*—indicative of the fact that emotions can sometimes cloud our better judgment. As a mental health professional, I am not immune to this dynamic. I'm a work in progress too. God isn't through with me yet!

How have these past intimate relationships affected you? Are you now extremely cautious about entering into relationships? What have you learned about yourself or the role you played in these relationships?

Just like anyone else that has been through a tumultuous, intimate relationship, I've had my share of difficulties with trust. I try to take people at face value for what they present to me. Sometimes my instincts to remain guarded have served me well, and likely saved me from additional hurt or heartache. Other times, I've allowed myself to trust people that didn't deserve it. I'm a *hope-ful* (but very realistic) romantic who still believes in love and the sanctity of marriage.

But sometimes it just doesn't work out and I've learned to be okay with that. My parents have been married for over 45 years, so I've seen partnership done well and I'm extremely grateful for that.

All in all, I'm certainly more perceptive of certain vices and habits that may be incompatible with my lifestyle. I've learned not to compromise my sense of self or my personal integrity because I won't have peace of mind in those relationships— (intimate, business, family, friendships, or any relationship otherwise.) My peace of mind is important to me, so I've certainly elected to remain single at times throughout my life versus being in a bad, unhealthy relationship. The biggest caution I have is in bringing anyone into my life that has an unsettled energy or lifestyle. I'm more aware of the potential for collateral damage, both to my children and myself.

So at this point in my life, I'm pretty selective about partnership and companionship.

One of things that stayed in the forefront of my mind while reading was how you learn to trust again. When you are presented with a new intimate relationship, how do you know it is safe to open your heart and soul again?

First and foremost, I wouldn't encourage going into a new relationship with the overwhelming thought of opening your heart and soul. That's like approaching Mount Everest thinking about how transformed and delivered you will feel once you've conquered it. The transformation and deliverance is a part of the greater process and is a byproduct of the overall journey, which we know is physically and emotionally arduous, requires great focus, preparation, and time. It requires you to literally stay in the moment with each step. Do your research on him. Be observant and diligent about getting to know him and his ways. Take your time.

With that said, let's take a closer look at the word *"trust"*. By definition, trust is a firm belief in the reliability, consistency, truth, or strength of someone or something. A firm belief. Establishing a firm belief takes time. Reliability and consistency are both concepts based on getting the same result repeatedly over time. Therefore, reliability and consistency take time. In relationships, (many people, including myself), have a tendency to believe what we see or hear at face value without a consistent demonstration of actions. It leads to feelings of vulnerability and ultimately a pattern of disappointment because of the invalidated *"trust"*.

Instead of putting your trust in others, I would encourage you to examine yourself. Do you have enough information about your new partner's reliability and consistency of behaviors, thoughts, and actions over time to establish a firm belief in them? In other words, trust is about *YOUR* beliefs based on the information you observe and collect over time. I encourage you to be observant, be diligent, and be patient before establishing a *firm belief and trust* in someone. Your instincts will tell you when it is safe. Don't be afraid to listen to your intuition.

Furthermore, part of my personal transformation over the years has included a fortified faith in God and scripture as a guide to manage any wavering anxieties when I'm faced with worldly issues. So biblically speaking, Proverbs 3:5 (NLT) says *"Trust in the Lord with all your heart; do not depend on your own understanding. Seek his will in all you do, and he will show you which path to take."* In this respect, if I were feeling a sense of uncertainty in a new relationship or any situation for that matter, a scriptural verse such as this would become a part of my daily meditation. Ultimately, it allows me to be mindful that if God doesn't have the relationship in His will for me, then it is not for me to worry about. — I trust Him. Regardless of one's spiritual or religious background, daily meditation, affirmations, and use of personal mantras are helpful in grounding anxieties in order to stay in the moment.

Do you worry about your girls having the "fix it" gene that will potentially put them in some poor relationships or keep them in those relationships longer than necessary?

I worry about women in general, (my girls included), trying to fix their husbands, brothers, and sons. Women are groomed to be nurturing, caregiving, and loyal to their husbands and children. This has a tendency to breed feelings of emotional exhaustion and resentment when they have given so much of themselves and the tank begins to run empty. They are left wondering: *Who's got my back? Why do I always have to do this or that?* I have all too often counseled women about the role they play in *caring too much* — leaving themselves depleted and their loved one handicapped from taking ownership for their own needs, wants, and desires. I'm a firm believer in personal accountability and each person taking responsibility for the role they play in their interactions with others.

Did your relationship with Janus affect your outlook on workplace romance?

I am fully aware that workplace romance has the tendency to be messy, so it's not something I recommend. But in a strange way, I think working with Janus may have actually helped the longevity of our relationship. Working with him each day allowed me to see him functional and well respected at work, versus only seeing him binge drinking at the end of the night. In this respect, our shared work kept glimpses of the part of him that I loved fresh in my mind. So, Janus and I were able to make it work. Sometimes, it was a little awkward in the aftermath of an incident that might have occurred the evening beforehand. In working together, there is the added pressure of splitting loyalties between colleagues or business associates if tension arises. We were able to keep the majority of our most personal affairs separate from the workplace. For those that did not know the ins and outs of our relationship, it came as quite a surprise that we ended in divorce.

There seems to be a fine line between a social drinker and a functional alcoholic. How does a loved one determine if their mate or loved one is truly an alcoholic?

Social drinkers tend to have a pretty low-risk drinking pattern. According to the National Institute on Alcohol Abuse and Alcoholism (NIAAA), "low-risk" drinking for females consists of no more than 7 drinks per week and no more than 3 drinks per sitting. For males, it consists of no more than 14 drinks per week and no more than 4 drinks per day. Although you are still subject for consequences, NIAAA research states that approximately 2% of drinkers within these limits develop an Alcohol Use Disorder. Functional alcoholics and "problem drinkers" have typically faced some negative consequences that elicit a need to cut back or cease drinking altogether. In the face of reasonable consequences, problem drinkers should be able to self-correct and adhere to social drinking responsibly.

In contrast, alcoholics may be given countless reasons to cut back on their drinking but are unable to permanently cut back — inevitably, returning to their alcoholic drinking patterns. One of the standard screening instruments for substance abuse, UNCOPE, first reported by Norman Hoffman and his colleagues in 1999, asks 6 questions that allows professionals to distinguish risk for substance abuse and dependence for alcohol and other drugs. Variations in wording are noted for several of the items.

U: "In the past year, have you ever drank or used drugs more than you meant to?" or, as revised "Have you spent more time drinking or using than you intended to?"

N: "Have you ever neglected some of your usual responsibilities because of using alcohol or drugs?"

C: "Have you felt you wanted or needed to cut down on your drinking or drug use in the last year?"

O: "Has anyone objected to your drinking or drug use?" Or, "Has your family, a friend, or anyone else ever told you they objected to your alcohol or drug use?"

P: "Have you ever found yourself preoccupied with wanting to use alcohol or drugs?" or, as revised, "Have you found yourself thinking a lot about drinking or using?"

E: "Have you ever used alcohol or drugs to relieve emotional discomfort, such as sadness, anger, or boredom?"

Scoring 2 or more positive responses indicates possible abuse, whereas scoring 4 or more positive responses indicates possible dependence. With either indication, I suggest seeking additional professional assessment and advice.

Do you think there was anything more you could have done to help Janus deal with his alcoholism? What would you suggest to someone who is living this same type of life?

Once my eyes were fully open to Janus' drinking habits, I believe I did everything I could as a wife to support him toward recognizing the impact of his drinking and get him help. I enlisted the support and opinion of his family, as they also had difficulties with his drunken tirades. My biggest concern, outside of his general health and safety, was how the drinking would affect our children. Once my concerns were established, the ultimate responsibility to do something about it was his. I decided that Janus' indecision to commit to sobriety was a *deal breaker* for me in the marriage.

> " $\mathcal{E}$stablish a boundary and clear understanding of what you will and will not be able to tolerate."

I would suggest anyone who is living in a similar situation to do the same. Establish a boundary and clear understanding of what you will and will not be able to tolerate. Think of a boundary as a personal, physical, and emotional fence that is built to make you feel safe. If someone keeps jumping over your fence, *or even worse, if someone keeps knocking down your fence*, you are responsible for imposing the consequences of feeling unsafe. Protect yourself. Otherwise, they will continue to invade your boundaries: your personal, physical, and emotional safety net.

Have Thony and Janus remained active in the girls' lives? Is Janus living sober?

Imani and I have not seen Thony since 2000 at her first birthday party. When she was 3 or 4 years old, I sent him a card, pictures, and update about her, but he never responded. He then sent her a birthday card when she turned 10 or 11 years old, to which we returned a card/letter hoping to jog some contact. Once again, there was no additional response. That has been the bulk of our direct interactions. We have kept contact with his family over the years, as his parents have provided financial and emotional support on his behalf. We've also had visits with them in recent years.

Janus is more available and engaged with the girls. He calls every so often and sends gifts during special occasions. Although he is only biologically linked to Erin, he has been involved with Imani since she was 5 years old. He treats them both equally, and for this reason, I have always carried a certain respect for him. Janus certainly expresses a desire to spend time with the girls, but they have not seen him in several years. Overall, we have a fairly cordial relationship and I am friendly with his family as well. As far as I know, he does not have a sober lifestyle, but I do not know the capacity to which he currently indulges in alcohol.

What tools have you used to get your children through all of the family changes intact and feeling loved?

I have the mindset that if children (in my case girls) aren't getting the love and attention they need, they will find it from somewhere else. — For example, they may find it in promiscuity, drugs, sports, gangs, etc. So, I heavily encourage channeling their quest to fill the void in a healthy fashion. For my girls, I consistently keep them active in sports and leisurely activities. I'm dedicated to have a schedule that allows me to be emotionally and physically available to them. This allows me to monitor them accordingly — from an emotionally, physically, and developmentally standpoint. — This allows me to stay on top of any wayward behaviors or emotions, given me the opportunity to resolve those issues at the early stage. I've also been blessed enough to foster a strong male presence in their lives through my father, brother, and God-brother. I'm intentional about surrounding them with other avenues of loving support through friendships, mine as well as theirs.

Professionally, the number one principle I emphasize for families going through separation/divorce is this: *"Children respond to the adults around them."* Separation and divorce is a difficult process. It can be emotionally, physically, and financially draining. Contentious arguing over custody, assets, money, and infidelity, in front of the children, adds fuel to the simmering coals. But overall, if the adults can get on the same page as not to convey any negative messages or overly emotional images to the children, they will respond better to the already difficult transition. There should be a united front, despite the apparent separation in the family.

As a therapist, I have been able to assist couples and families through the separation and divorce process, whether it is to mediate the marital relationship or to move toward successful co-parenting and divorce. So, seeking therapy is a good step if you, as the adult, are having a hard time managing your emotional reactions in front of the children. You should also seek therapy if you recognize any emotional conflict in the children. In addition, check your local resources for support groups catering to children of separation and divorce.

Conversation Three

Pure

Pure

is a modern twist on Puer aeternus, a Latin term

used in mythology to refer to an older man whose

emotional life has remained at an adolescent level.

In modern psychology, the puer struggles to face

life and its responsibilities and often has an

unhealthy dependence on the mother.

My oldest brother is a crack-head. It's an ugly, derogatory term. I could certainly sugarcoat this and deliver it with honey, but I won't. Crack cocaine brought a raw and gritty addiction, which I imagine has taken him to the deepest and darkest places of his psyche, self-worth, and dignity. I wouldn't wish that fate on my worst enemy, let alone my brother. But I've witnessed and been a part of his struggle with depression and drug addiction since I was a teenager. I don't know whether the chicken or the egg came first, and after nearly 30 years of his downward spiral, it doesn't really matter. Nothing can change the fact that an overwhelming majority of my brother's life has been spent addicted to crack-cocaine, which has taken my family on a long and tawdry journey.

My earliest memories of Pure's addiction were when I was in middle school. I was going steady with my best friend's cousin. He was one of my first middle school boyfriend's, and he let me wear his gold chain. It had a charm with his initials or a nameplate of some kind. He made me swear to take care of it because it was real gold, and he would get in trouble if it were lost or broken. I was so proud to wear it. I took it off each night, placing it on my dresser, as I had promised. I woke one morning to find it missing. I was oblivious to what was going on with Pure, and I tore my room upside down and inside out looking for it. He saw me crying and asked what the matter was. Once I told him, he said he'd look for it while I was at school. Of course, it never resurfaced. My parents paid to replace that loss and others, over and over again. I could rewrite the story line for that incident a thousand times.

All I'd need to do is interchange the stolen item. There have been countless televisions, DVD players, cameras, engagement rings, wedding rings, and gold chains stolen from various family members. There have been emptied wallets, purses, piggy banks, and bank accounts. I'm all too familiar with being consumed by a massive wave of shock, anger, and repeated disappointment when I've discovered that something was missing. The cumulative thousands of dollars of stolen property doesn't compare to the emotional cost of feeling like a victim in one's own home. But in this case, it wasn't an estranged thief in the night I worried about; it was my brother. We grew up in the same home playing baseball and break dancing in the living room. I hadn't the slightest inkling he, or anyone else in my family, would steal from me. I was blindsided by his betrayal.

At times, the flagrancy of stealing behind my back, or right from under my nose, was replaced with the pity-laden request for $20. "Until I get paid on Friday," he said. Friday never came. In fact, Pure was often not employed long enough to receive more than a couple paychecks. In the world of addiction, money is as much a poison as the drug itself. Job after job was gained and lost within a matter of weeks, or maybe a few months. With a high school equivalency diploma and limited job skills, finding a job for a black man with a criminal record was far from easy. So being able to find an employer to give him a chance was a gift that seemed to be an inevitable avenue toward the slippery slope of relapse.

Pure's addiction also included the "Can I borrow your car real quick?" storyline. Or even worse, I'd wake up in the morning to go to school or work to find my car missing. This typically resulted in a 2-3 day absence from the house, followed by a call from the police about an abandoned car, a moving violation, or a public disturbance of some kind. If not arrested and jailed, he'd eventually take the walk of shame back into the house. The pattern was pretty textbook: drug binge, stolen items from around our house or neighborhood, fired from a job, borrowed money from several family members (usually with an accompanying sob story to pull at their heart strings), arrested, and customarily retreated to the cave-dwelling of his bedroom.

Whatever he and my parents discussed after they bailed him out of jail or refinanced the house to support his legal bills was not discussed in front of me. Pure was the pink elephant in the room. My mother would languish in thought over the actions of her oldest child, seeming to retreat to her bedroom in a parallel state of sadness and worry for her son. With each arrest or stolen item, she was equally annoyed and disheartened, wanting to believe that he was merely in the wrong place at the wrong time. And even when she knew he was in the wrong, she never wanted him to feel abandoned. As disappointing as it may have seemed, she rescued him, time and time again, and was a faithful and compassionate mother to the detriment of her heavy heart. It was hard to see her loyalty constantly tested and manipulated by Pure's wayward lifestyle and damaged mindset. In retrospect, I believe it may have brought us closer together as mother and daughter. I grew to understand her heart, whether I agreed with her actions or not.

During my late teens, I wondered if it would be easier if he were dead. I didn't want him to suffer nor did I wish him any harm, but in his death I thought there would be peace. If this were the case, I wouldn't have to worry, be angry, or hate him for all the broken promises and countless boldface lies. For a while, I was so embarrassed and disgusted with him that I basically denied his existence. Some of my closest friends didn't know about him. He was 6 years older than me and always incognito, either in jail, rehab, or simply missing in action. It wasn't hard to act as if he were a non-factor and non-existent.

My closest brother, KJ, was 3 years older than I. We both thrived in school and athletics in our local community; therefore, Pure's presence (or lack thereof), was easily overshadowed and disregarded. He was supposed to be the big brother. He was supposed to lead the way for us all, but his path was significantly derailed. In his absence, life went on as usual. My mother and father were faithful cheerleaders and coaches, on the sidelines of every sporting event or activity we had. From bowling to gymnastics to basketball to football to long exhausting sun-scorching summer track meets, they were always there. Our family camaraderie and togetherness did not falter, and perhaps may have been propelled by Pure's thread of addiction. In this respect, it was easier if he stayed away. We may have been "*minus one*" in numbers, but we were overall resilient in our daily stride. We didn't have to hide our jewelry or latest gadgets. There was an increased sense of personal and emotional security in his absence.

KJ went on to play Division-I college football in Chicago studying biomedical engineering. I earned 12 varsity letters in my high school sports career before accepting a full-academic scholarship to West Virginia University. What an awkward juxtaposition for a parent, two children in college and the third in jail or rehab. This was our reality. During an occasional phone call, Pure verbalized feelings of pride for KJ and I, but I'm sure our accolades didn't reflect well on his self-worth. I imagine the "If I shoulda, coulda, woulda's" swirling in his head, which perhaps served as more fuel for the addiction. Upon release from some stint of jail or rehab during my freshman year of college, we had professional family portraits taken for the first time in about 15 years. My mother was happy to have all of her children and family reunited in that moment.

I spent two academic years at WVU before transferring my credits to a school in Maryland. My parents, ever supportive of my decisions, took me in, which they have done several times throughout my early adulthood. I returned to the comfort of my childhood home, got a full-time job, and commuted to University of Maryland in Baltimore County, where I studied developmental psychology and sociology. Other times, I moved back home on the heels of divorce and having children. They never judged me or questioned my actions. They have been my backbone when I needed stability and were as supportive as any family could be. When I returned to school for my Master's and Doctorate degrees, they were essentially the other parent for my girls in absence of their fathers. I am forever grateful and appreciative of their support, but their goodness has sometimes felt like a gift and a curse.

My parents' unconditional compassion for Pure has been a source of contention. He was allowed to lie, cheat, steal, and make us all feel like victims in our home, but he always had a place to lay his head. Although this can be seen as a valiant demonstration of unconditional parental love, it doesn't feel so warm and fuzzy when your feelings and personal belongings are in jeopardy. So as much as I love and enjoy my parents, living with them meant living with him. Living with him meant leaving myself, and my children, exposed to his drama. On a good day, he laughed, joked, and was silly with the rest of the family. On an average day, he was isolated in his room, making an occasional appearance to use the bathroom or get something to eat. But more often than not, living with Pure meant sleeping with my purse and car keys under my pillow. Living with Pure meant explaining to my preteen daughter that she had to keep track of her Nintendo DS and her leftover lunch money. Living with Pure and his roller coaster of addiction was not much different than living with someone with a mood disorder or someone who suffered with alcoholism. Either way I looked at it, I was strapped in for the ride on his emotional rollercoaster.

In his adult life, currently in his mid-forties, Pure has probably spent a cumulative total of 5 years living productively and gainfully employed outside of my parent's home. The other years have been occupied by multiple incarcerations, halfway houses, drug treatment programs, and a few months of homelessness when my parents refused to let him stay in the house. The pattern of his addiction and their rescuing of him fostered some of my frustration. As much as I love and respect them, I often questioned how they could continue to allow him into the home. I didn't understand the internal conflict they must've felt. All I knew for sure was that I didn't want to live with Pure…but it wasn't my house. I tried to convince them to put him out. It shouldn't have taken much coercing because his actions spoke volumes about his state of mind and the severity of his addiction. But you can't force anyone into recovery, any more than you can force a parent to contribute to her child's homelessness.

My mother has been uneasy for years, feeling like she has had to choose between her children. To this day, she continues to struggle over supporting him unconditionally at the cost of her other two children. She is one of my best friends, and my girls love her beyond measure, so she won't lose us either way. But, I recall being bound and determined to move out of my parents' house whether I could fully afford it or not. KJ had long reestablished himself in Northern Virginia, away from our childhood home. Neither of us wanted to be in the line of fire, exposed, and vulnerable to his addictive behaviors. It's interesting being a part of a family that is so intrinsically and genuinely connected, yet there is such a fundamentally strained fiber of addiction.

Over the years, I've had to establish pretty clear boundaries about my refusal to support Pure financially. This includes contributing to bail, legal fees, replacing stolen items, etc. If my parents wanted him in the house, they had to face the consequences of his presence. I have given my opinion from time to time, and other family members have done so also, but ultimately it seemed to fall on deaf ears. If my parents, specifically my mother, felt inclined to collect money for bail, legal fees, or commissary, I always refused to be a part of it. Nor would I pay their bills so that they can focus their income on him. I don't wish to support him by proxy. If they want to support him, they will do it on their own dime in their own house. KJ and I are pretty consistent in that feeling.

Through the years of pain and betrayal, I've come to recognize the best way to support Pure is in prayer. I will consistently ask God to free him of his vulnerabilities and lift the burden of anguish that I've had toward him throughout my life. I will always reinforce his sobriety and pray for his self-preservation. When he is clean and emotionally available in my presence, I will hug him as my brother just the same. During periods of homelessness when he has called me for money to get something to eat, I brought him food. When he has asked me for gas money, I put gas in his car. In fact, I don't recall the last time I actually put money directly into his hands. I don't trust him with money and will consistently refrain from giving it to him because I know his weakness. I refuse to take part in "feeding the beast" we call addiction. My mother, on the other hand, will give him her last $10 if it means he will stop begging her for it. His weakness is her weakness.

It's difficult to watch her brokenhearted over the iniquities of her oldest child. She has a strong desire to believe that each rock bottom will be the last rock bottom; but it only seems to be followed by another rock bottom. She wants to see him at peace and ultimately feels she has some control over that. She blames herself for his addiction. She blames herself for moving from one neighborhood to the next where he had difficulty adjusting and got caught up in the "wrong crowd" 30 years ago. She blames herself and feels overwhelmed with the need to bear his cross.

My mother is blinded by a mother's love. A blindness that won't allow her to cut the umbilical cord of a grown man. She is deafened to his drug-infused lies, excuses, and fairytales, "I know you think I'm always defending him, but I'm really not sure he did it this time." *This time? As opposed to the other 40 or 50 times he's been charged and apprehended?* To which, KJ and I shake our heads and sigh with confusion wondering what "bad luck" befell him *this time*. She is often his lone ear and advocate as he tries to redeem himself from yet another sordid circumstance. Any actual truth he shares is stranded in the murky waters of timeless deceit.

She's blinded by a mother's responsibility. Responsibility that allows her to repeatedly and unconsciously enable him and cater to his exhausting requests. She enables him to be dependent on others, particularly herself. Imagine 30 years of repeated requests for money, sob stories about why he lost his job, excuses about how he's being mistreated by someone, and the relentless requests, like "Can you take me to..." There's also a never ending stockpile of "I'm sorry" and "Why me" and "Can you just…" This was continuous year after year after year. When everyone else has grown tired of being hurt and the bridge is all but ashes, my mother has been ever faithful to Pure, even though he has not been loyal to her.

> "*A man without a sense of responsibility is limited in his demonstration of manhood.*"

It has to be exhausting to give and give and give, with every hope that your giving will result in *this time* being *the last time*. At some point, the giving seemed to be in vain because she was so blinded by the truth. Where the rest of us have felt depleted, she has not broken her commitment to him. For that, I marvel at my mother's complicated delivery of love, compassion, and resilience to care for Pure without fail. Because I promise you this: If you didn't already know her relationship with Pure, you would never know her relationship with Pure. You would never know there was a thread of codependency between them that has seemed to cripple him from establishing his own initiative for responsibility. *A man without a sense of responsibility is limited in his demonstration of manhood.* Maybe she feels like he can't handle the responsibility, so she carries the burden to shield him from further disappointment and frustration that would encourage his addiction. It is a flawed, very tangled web they have weaved. Her blindness is well intentioned, but it is blindness nonetheless.

My mother is comforted having her family together, so she is not short of effort to keep us in contact with Pure. "It would be nice if you sent him a letter or something". KJ and I have been known to soothe her suggestions from time to time through the years, but for the most part our contacts are limited to encounters at my parent's house either by collect call from jail, or when he is home on parole/probation. When the three of us are in the same room, it's not obvious that there has been decades of lying, stealing, and emotional roller coasters. We laugh incessantly. We actually reminisce about old childhood memories. Before the drugs, we played football together in the living room, climbed trees in the woods behind our house, and went fishing with our dad. We fought with each other and *for* each other as siblings do. We grew up watching the same TV shows, so we have a lot of inside jokes that prompt a domino effect of chuckles between us. We have very enjoyable family dinners without incident. But at the end of the day, I don't trust Pure outside of my eyesight. I'm not sure if I'll ever be able to trust him, for which I am unapologetic. When visiting my parents, I will continue to hide my belongings, keep my purse within arm's reach, and tell my daughter to hold on to her iPod. Forgiveness is one thing. Trust is another.

Living with a drug addict throughout my life and staying one step ahead of his fiendish behaviors has become a way of life I'm accustomed to in my parent's home. I can't divorce him. I can't put an end to his addiction. I can't make my parents stop supporting him. By blood and circumstance, I'm forever bound to him and his addiction. I'm a passenger on Pure's rollercoaster with my eyes wide open.

Necessary Conversation #3

The subject of being co-dependent always comes to mind when talking about alcoholism or addiction. Can you explain codependency more clearly?

Codependent relationships are common in alcoholism and drug addiction. Codependency is a well-intentioned but dysfunctional manner of interacting with the substance abuser that ultimately fuels the addiction and the addictive behavior. There is often an overreliance on someone or several people to enable the behavior and/or maintain the secretive nature of the behavior. This can be done by funding the addiction, turning a blind eye to the behavior, making excuses for the behavior, or by passively allowing the addiction to persist.

In codependent relationships there is often very poor boundaries and an exaggerated sense of responsibility to *"rescue"* the loved one. Mental Health America (MHA) describes the helpers as having a need to feel needed, in which they may keep the loved one close and dependent out of a fear of abandonment or loss. Whereas the help-receiving addict has been impeded in maturity, life skills, or confidence that further fuels their dependence on the helper. It fulfills needs of being taken care of, feeling loved, and receiving concern from the helper, which ultimately impedes the motivation for change. Codependency is an unhealthy relationship pattern that can be difficult to recognize for those entrenched in the situation.

Do you feel that your experiences with your brother, and the boundaries that you worked to set there, helped you when navigating the situation with Janus?

My attempts to curb Janus' drinking habits felt all too familiar. Just as in my relationship with Pure, it was a harsh reality to recognize that I had zero to no control over his drinking but was still vulnerable to his actions. I had to establish boundaries to protect my children and myself. As Imani began to unwittingly recognize signs of intoxication and his pattern of binge drinking/hangovers, I was mortified by the idea of raising my children in an alcoholic home. According to the American Association of Marriage and Family Therapy (AAMFT), children with alcoholic parents are more likely to experience symptoms of anxiety and/or depression, antisocial behavior, relationship difficulties, and/or behavioral problems. They have a higher risk for alcoholism and other drug abuse, compared to children of non-alcoholics, and are more likely to marry an alcoholic as well. In this sense, a generational cycle of addiction becomes perpetuated and infused in the family system. And there I was, living the cycle. I grew up privy to the relationship of co-dependency between my mother and brother. I rejected the idea of minimizing Janus' drinking and covering up things in the aftermath. I was ill with resentment and frustration with each surmounting occurrence of intoxication. I didn't want my children bearing witness to my emotional upset, nor his intoxication. It was a generational pattern I was not willing to repeat amongst my children. So I decided it was my responsibility to shield them from the likelihood of repeating a generational curse.

You primarily talk about your mother's enabling and rescuing of your brother, but what about your father? What was his role in all of it?

In this situation, my father, is best described as an *enabler by proxy*. When it came to my brother, my perspective is that my dad wanted to support my mother's initiative to fight for Pure, but not necessarily make any major requests on his behalf. So whereas my mother was a relentless advocate drumming up money or defending him (despite the imposing guilt of his actions), my father was a passive buffer. I think he felt that it may not have been worth the fight with his wife or the addiction. There were times when he certainly played the "*heavy*" delivering the news that Pure had to leave the house, but I think he wanted to support my mother's feelings more than anything.

Was your father active in the home and in raising you?

Yes, he was very active in my life. After retiring from corporate America, my father was a full-time teacher in physical education and weight training at the high school that my siblings and I attended. We grew up under his athletic expertise playing and participating in various sports, which he often coached: football, basketball, bowling, weight training, as well as track and field. He also has a very enthusiastic, adventurous attitude. So he took us on fishing trips and a lot of family outings to amusement parks and such. My father is a charismatic, very well-liked, and respected figurehead in the local community. He's been quite active in the development of many student-athletes that progressed to college athletics and beyond. His presence in my life is one of those things I've always been privileged to have, so I didn't fully recognize the larger impact of it until I was older. He also has been quite a presence for my daughters throughout the years. I'm grateful for the example he and my brother KJ have been to my girls.

Have your parents ever sought counseling or support groups to assist them in understanding Pure's addiction?

As far as I remember, we all participated in some family counseling when Pure was in a rehabilitation center as a late adolescent. But I think that was the only time. There was at least one other occasion that I suggested a support group to my mother, but to my knowledge, it never happened. There have also been times where she would ask my professional opinion of things as if she was trying to understand the addiction, the legal process, or help-seeking on Pure's behalf.

What effect has your relationship with Pure had on your relationship with your parents? Has it strained your relationship in any way? Is your brother viewed as the "taboo" subject causing feelings of anger and resentment when he is discussed between yourself and parents? If so, how can this be healed?

As I stated in Pure's story, I have a very close, tight-knit family. The strand of dysfunction and addiction that is woven through it is exceedingly overshadowed by genuine care, affection, and a camaraderie of love and support. My friends, extended family, and people that know us personally often comment on the warm relationships we have. So that's what makes Pure's story even more difficult to fathom.

He is easily the *"taboo"* subject between my parents, namely my mother, and myself; but when the subject is apparent there is no shying away from it. KJ and I are aligned in position on the matter because of our perspective on it, which allows us to talk about it more openly than others I suppose. My mother has a tendency to dance around it from time to time because she thinks we "don't care". But that's not the case. We just fundamentally disagree on how to manage it.

Out of the 3 conversations, Pure's story is the most *"unfinished"* because he continues to struggle with addiction and the illegal behaviors surrounding his drug use. He is also the most prevalent character in my life in comparison to my exes, who are pretty much estranged. He is presently incarcerated facing a significant sentence for violating his probation. Once again, KJ and I had to confront my mother about the enabling behaviors. So there was a fairly recent "*intervention*" amongst the family members involved. I believe it contributes to the healing process both for her individually and for the family as a whole. Also, I believe this book will be therapeutic reading as well. I have spoken with Pure directly about his role in this book. He has mixed feelings about our story being shared. At times, he has been understanding, while other times he feels vilified and unnecessarily exposed. My hope is that it may jog some insight and healing energy.

Conversation Four

A Vision To Decide

A Vision To Decide

"Eyes blinded by the fog of things cannot see truth.

Ears deafened by the din of things cannot hear truth.

Brains bewildered by the whirl of things cannot think truth.

Hearts deadened by the weight of things cannot feel truth.

Throats choked by the dust of things cannot speak truth."

Harold Bell Wright
The Uncrowned King (1910)

How do I know for sure if I'm a blind passenger?
What are the signs?

blind passenger is likely to experience the highs and lows along with their loved one. So in identifying the signs of a blind passenger, you also have to consider the signs and symptoms of instability in the loved one.

Imagine your loved one has bipolar disorder, which is characterized with mood swings between depression and mania. They may be prone to a lack of sleep—either because they can't sleep or won't sleep. Restlessness may lead them to hang out all hours of the night, have racing thoughts, engage in drinking/ drugging excessively, and have mood swings. In this state, he or she may have grand ideas, to start a new company, business, or invention. With a high or "*manic*" phase, they might be more fun to be around. There's a playful spontaneity that can be exciting and energizing. It's not uncommon for people with bipolar disorder to go on shopping sprees in which inordinate amounts of money are spent. The excessive spending can have a detrimental impact on a family's finances and has the potential to cost just as much to repair. Imagine bank accounts overdrawn and credit cards maxed out leaving major financial ruin. As the blind passenger in this scenario, you may feel exhausted, frustrated, and heavily annoyed trying to tether their frenzied energy and zest for life.

The highs of addiction come with a relentless passion for self-gratification. This includes acting on an addictive surge of compulsive thoughts and behaviors with minimal regard for consequences or the feelings of others. There's a persistent dedication to drink, get high, watch pornography, have sex, gamble, or eat in an excessive and unreasonable fashion. Depending on the addiction of choice, there may be repeated requests for money, absences from work, memory lapses, unfulfilled responsibilities, and a concentrated effort to hide or lie about the behaviors. The slightest suggestion that things are getting out of control are denied or minimized, which is a hallmark feature of addiction—better known as denial. Eventually, the blame game sets in: *"You're no fun"* or *"It's your fault for nagging me."* As a blind passenger, there's a profound feeling that the addict is being selfish. You may feel obliged to reason with them, to leash the highness of their inflated beliefs and out of control behaviors. If it feels like it's too much, it usually is. But addicts are sometimes too far-gone to respond to logic.

To the other extreme, there are lows that accompany addiction and mental illness as well. There is a "*crash*" in the sense of emotional and physical fatigue, self-pity, disparaging thoughts, and low self-esteem. This is typically where a guilty conscience sets in and the overwhelming feeling of being a burden to others can lend way to suicidal ideas, thoughts, and actions. As a blind passenger, you may feel stuck between a wealth of feelings. There may be anger or resentment for the damage caused to the relationship. You may feel exhausted for constantly having to attend to the emotional, physical, and financial needs of someone else. You may feel anxious and hurried to fix it or make the mental illness/addiction secede. You're merely looking for relief and the freedom of not having to worry–anymore. If the situation isn't addressed, it becomes a shared experience of depression and despair.

The *crash* amidst an addiction also includes a *"cleanup phase,"* whereby the blind passenger may have to repair any destroyed property, pick up a stolen car, or perhaps clean up vomit amongst other things. This also includes the financial repercussions of hiring an attorney or initiating treatment for the identified problem. In the face of chronic addiction, broken promises are par for the course. Another "I'm sorry" is added to the stockpile of apologies and relapses. There are feelings of hopelessness and doubt for whether sustained recovery is possible.

What coping mechanisms or strategies do 'blind passengers' need to keep in mind as they try to live through their situations with loved ones going through addiction, mental illness, and/or alcoholism?

The hallmark feature of being a blind passenger is that you fail to truly identify and pinpoint the emotional instability and/or addiction of a loved one as he/she elicits a rollercoaster of experiences that impact you, your friends, and your family. It essentially becomes a shared trauma amongst the loved ones who bear witness to and are a part of the sordid journey. As the ups and downs become a *"normal"* part of your relationship, you have wants, needs, hopes, and desires that take a backseat to the addiction or mental illness and all of the accompanying difficulties. The addict, alcoholic, or mentally ill loved one is the primary figure involved, but they are often too mired in a state of denial, delusion, habit, or depletion to make the lifestyle changes that will offer you a relief. This is the most important distinction to consider: YOUR relief and the things you want in that moment may be quite different then the relief they desire, if they desire a relief at all.

As you exhaust a wealth of energy trying to get them to understand what you want and how you feel, they are emotionally ill equipped to do anything about it. So here is the ultimate thought for every blind passenger to ponder as they find themselves veiled with confusion, resentment, anger, sadness, and exhaustion: *"If you have a loved one who is struggling to be responsible for his or her own thoughts and feelings, what makes you think they are capable of responding accordingly to yours?"* Can you embrace the fact that the confusion, resentment, anger, sadness, and sense of depletion you feel is your responsibility regardless of its catalyst? In short, will you decide to take responsibility for your own emotional health? Here are some specific points to consider as you seek a clearer vision and perspective to make decisions about your situation.

Ownership

You need to begin separating YOUR journey on this emotional rollercoaster from THEIR journey of instability. You're exhausted, frustrated, disappointed, and at your wits end trying to wrangle what you've identified as *the problem*. Your hope has grown futile and you're feeling defeated that things are unchanged, or potentially getting worse. The frustration and disappointment you feel is due to being intimately linked to the volatility of the shared issue, but you are now enmeshed in the dynamics

> " *You need to begin separating your journey on this emotional rollercoaster from their journey of instability.* "

of the problem. This may be a harsh reality for some of you to grasp as you are passionately and unconditionally dedicated toward "*helping*" your loved one. But at the end of the day, it is YOUR job to manage and YOUR emotions, just as it is THEIR job to manage THEIRS.

If you have found yourself in a daze or otherwise emotionally distracted and stressed out, then it is clear that neither of you are in a healthy space. What you're feeling is a byproduct of the original source of instability (a loved one's addiction, mental illness, mood swings, emotional tirades, alcoholism, obsessive behaviors, etc.); but you are now a part of the problem. If you are not already exhausted, you will become it. Under those circumstances, you are not the best source of help for them. Your feelings, wants, needs, and resentments will get in the way of your ability to help them. Hence, you need to take ownership for your feelings and your emotional state in order to get the clarity and relief you need. The goal is to bring a healthier, more emotionally available version of you to the relationship.

Boundaries

Accepting ownership for the role you are playing in the situation allows a better look at the boundary issues that lie between you and your loved one. Relationship boundaries are an invisible dividing line built to establish safety and responsibility in your interactions with others. It's the understanding we have with one another, *spoken or unspoken*, that make the distinction between what is comfortable or favorable to you, and what is not. I could write a whole book about boundaries on its own, but for the purposes of this context, consider this analogy:

In life, we each have a proverbial plate of food. On that plate are all of life's necessities to aid in us in becoming a fully nourished, well-balanced person. In our relationships and interactions with others, we have a tendency to share food. We learned as children that *"sharing is caring"* in a healthy, cooperative relationship, it is. But in unhealthy situations, the proverbial sharing can be toxic and foster a pattern of codependency. Codependent sharing happens in many ways. Here are a few examples:

- By invitation: "Hey I don't want all of this, do you want some?"
- By feelings of obligation or responsibility: "You're my child so I have to take care of that for you."

- By imposition of guilt: "If you really loved me you would do this for me."
- By manipulation: "No one else is helping me, so…"
- By feelings of inadequacy: "I don't know how to eat all of this."

The *list of examples* are endless, but the final result is the same: *"In codependent, toxic relationships there is a consistent sharing of the 'food' that is required for one to be a fully nourished, well-balanced person."*

"*In codependent, toxic relationships there is a consistent sharing of the 'food' that is required for one to be a fully nourished, well-balanced person."*

Without a full plate of food, someone is left undernourished, empty, and ill equipped to manage life's stressors independently, and are consistently seeking a loved one to fill the void. It is one thing to teach, build up, provide, and support someone. It's another thing to do it for them, excuse them, enable them, allow them, and essentially get in the way of them spending the time, energy, and personal fortitude to do it for themselves. When they are feeling inadequate, vulnerable, or just plain tired, they ask, passive-aggressively expect, and sometimes demand for you to take it off their plate. And as long as they are not taught, encouraged, supported, and required to "*eat*" all that is necessary for them to be a fully nourished, well-balanced person, they will not be a fully nourished, well-balanced person. They will always feel vulnerable, inadequate, dependent, and incomplete. They will consistently be in search of someone or something to take the food off their plate.

And when you, *the blind passenger*, take on someone else's "leftovers", time and time again, adding them to your plate, which is already filled with your necessities… *So, guess who gets full, overwhelmed, fatigued, and obese with resentment?* Although I want to believe this dynamic is built out of the best of intentions, it is nonetheless a faulty interaction that feeds the complexities of unhealthy relationships.

Taking ownership for the role you play in the tangled, unhealthy web of emotional, physical, and sometimes financial dependency, allows you to reestablish boundaries. With new boundaries, you can begin to eliminate the exhaustive overuse of your resources, time, energy, and feelings, and subsequently return the other responsibility and ownership to the appropriate plate. When you redefine the boundary of responsibility, it allows for personal accountability in the relationship. Personal accountability in the relationship puts you and your loved one in a situation to get the help you each need as individuals, instead of relying on each other to take care of the other's feelings. That's not working.

> " *Do not get stuck in the thought that you're the only person that can help them.*"

New boundaries will relieve you of holding the overwhelming responsibility of someone else's battle. Separate your needs from those of the original problem and take care of you. This may mean physical separation from the source of instability in the way of a respite visit away from the home or to move out of the house altogether. Perhaps it means one or both of you needs a rehabilitative substance abuse treatment, a crisis bed, or a therapeutic regimen.

Once you are able to clear some of the cobwebs that accumulate with the daily regimentation of being connected with an unstable person, it allows for some relief and clarity. It makes the roles of ownership more distinct. For example, if you have a spouse who is a heavy drinker, you will have a tendency to scrutinize, manage, and react to any presence of drinking. In essence, you are playing the role of spouse, substance abuse counselor, police, and *"single"* parent, if there are children present. The compounded stress of playing multiple roles in attempt to tether a spouse is exhausting! Do not get stuck in the thought that you're the only person that can help them.

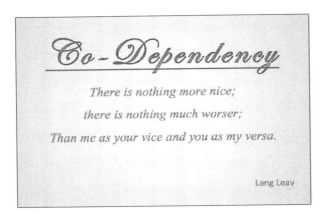

You cannot be the spouse and the substance abuse counselor. Your job is to be the spouse. As much as you would love to get them sober, put them on medication, demand them into recovery, or make them talk to a professional; the primary ownership for their care belongs to them. You can only help those who want to help themselves. If they do not have a clear commitment toward treatment and lifestyle management, you will consistently feel as you do. You need to take care of your feelings and your needs separate from them in order to gain clarity and perspective on the situation.

Get Educated

As you begin to recognize the source of your distress, you should take action to educate yourself accordingly. You need to know as much as possible about the situation. For example: If a medical doctor diagnosed your spouse with diabetes, you would need to gain a better understanding of the diet, exercise, and medication regimen required to manage the condition. You would familiarize yourself with the signs of having a blood sugar count that is too high, or too low. You would buy and prepare food in accordance with dietary guidelines for diabetes. You would become familiar with the side effects of medication and be attentive to any changes in your spouse. Well, mental and emotional health carries the same level of understanding and attention.

Get educated about any mental health or substance abuse diagnoses that may be at the source of your relationship woes. Seek the expertise of a professional that may be able to help you identify with what is going on with your loved one. Sometimes we are quick to say, *"You need help,"* when we see a loved one struggling with erratic behaviors and feelings. But as you're begging and pleading for them to get help, the problem persists. I'm encouraging you to seek information and clarity with or without them.

Whether its bipolar disorder, binge drinking, anger issues, an eating disorder, or substance abuse, you need to understand what you are a part of and come to the realization that the experience you're having is not happening by accident. Professional and reliable information keeps you from being stuck in your head wondering, worrying, and feeling confused. Information and facts validates the worries and feelings in your head, and brings them to a more realistic, tangible status—with a name, symptoms, recommendations, and prognosis. Information allows for clarity and therefore initiates problem solving and decision-making. Also, seeking professional information keeps your privacy in tact when you are too embarrassed, uncertain, or too proud to talk with your family about what you're going through.

Safety

I am fully aware what it feels like to be in an unhealthy relationship. Sometimes my thoughts were extremely clouded. I was confused. I tried to tell myself it was *"gonna be okay"*. I was embarrassed and ashamed to be a part of some of the things that were happening and I didn't know exactly what to do. And even amidst a domestically violent dispute with my husband, I never had the thought in my mind to call the police. I was bleeding from my forehead with impending bruises on my arms and legs, but it never crossed my mind to call for help. In retrospect, I think I just needed someone to plant the seed in my head because I was too foggy to derive the thought on my own. So here is the seed I plant for you… ***"If you are feeling unsafe at any time, call someone."***

Your safety is paramount. Call the police, a crisis hotline, a therapist, a domestic violence shelter, a friend, a family member, a clergyman/pastor, or knock on the neighbor's door. When harm or danger is at stake, there is no time to be *blinded* by pride or to be worried about being the subject of tomorrow's gossip. It is best to air on the side of caution and call someone. Keeping the fact that you're in an unhealthy, unsafe situation to yourself is a road to more misery, and will only contribute to further demise. As I began reaching out to others about my situation with Thony, it became real. It was no longer a shameful story stuck inside my head. When the time came, I was able to be more decisive about my direction. Get out of your own head and tell someone. If you don't have a friend or family member that has your safety and best interests at heart, then I encourage you to seek sources that are *wise, worthy and supportive.* Be relentless in making a decision about your safety.

Along the same line of safety, I encourage you to think about your overall emotional health. Sometimes people remain in an unhealthy situation because there is no prevalent danger at hand. But the long term implications of exposing yourself to a stressful situation or toxic relationship is dangerous to your emotional health, and has a lasting impact on all other relationships in your life.

One of my favorite therapeutic mantras, which I often pose to clients, is this: *There is always something comfortable about the uncomfortable situations in which we remain.* What comfortable thoughts or ideas are you holding onto that seemingly outweigh the discomfort of your situation? Consciously or unconsciously, people have a tendency to wager one unhealthy situation against another. I saw this struggle prevalent in my mother. She was being torn between enabling the drug habits, homelessness, and related illegal behaviors of her oldest son versus that of consistently healthy home for her other two children, absent of Pure. I believe she was comfortable (but still uncomfortable) with the idea that she was supporting him and couldn't bear the thought of him being homeless, even if it made the immediate situation of allowing him to come back in the house uncomfortable.

This dynamic is also seen in those that will remain in an abusive relationship as not to disrupt the kids. In essence, you've decided to expose your kids to an example of an unhealthy, abusive, and emotionally damaged relationship versus that of a separated family. Neither is ideal; but which one has the greater potential for health, safety, and stability? Please consider the vision or ideas you have for your future self and the future of your family as long as you're living in an unsafe environment.

Health and safety was a pivotal driving force in my vision to decide to separate in my marriages, and again in moving out of my parent's home as an adult. They were by no means "*easy*" choices to make. But the vision for my future did not allow me to see myself in a physically and emotionally abusive marriage in front of my daughter. I did not want to imagine either of my daughters witnessing or directly experiencing anything that had the potential to damage their vision for their own future. Without a partner with the same vision, I decided I was not willing to raise children in an unhealthy and harmful marriage because I feared the prognosis for a healthy future was in jeopardy.

Let Go Of The Outcome

One of the biggest difficulties we have in making decisions for ourselves, and our families, is that we are holding on to the outcome we desire with and for the other person. You want them to go to therapy or stop using drugs or stop being unfaithful. You want them to understand how they are hurting you so that things can be "*normal*". You just want them to be reasonable and stop whatever they are doing to upset you. In reestablishing some boundaries and separating yourself from the original source of instability, you begin to realize that you have no control over what is bringing you turmoil, which means you have *no* control of the outcome. So it's time to let go of the ideal outcome you have in your head, and start getting mentally and emotionally prepared to take the next step to help your situation.

I remember thinking that if I refused to let any alcohol in the house that my husband, Janus, would stop drinking and I would feel better. So what happened? He stopped drinking *in the house*. It didn't stop him from drinking outside of the house and stumbling in fully intoxicated smelling like a brewery. I was pleading with him, trying to get him to understand how I felt, how it was killing our family, and how frustrated and disgusted I was. I thought to myself, "Surely he will hear my pleas and stop drinking." Before long I realized that my pleas were falling on deaf, alcoholic ears and that I had ZERO control over whether he decided to stop drinking. Which means I had very little control of what my interactions with my husband would be each day. I had the idea of a content, loving marriage but my house did not feel like a home. I was uncomfortable because of the uncertainty of his binge drinking and the potential difficulties that could befall each night. Having no insight, foresight, or control over his condition limited the possibilities of my ability to plan for a better future with him.

In order for me to find some degree of comfort and control in my marriage, I had to let go of what I believed was the most desirable outcome — for him to stop drinking. In my eyes, his drinking was the catalyst for our marital difficulties, because if and when he was sober I had peace of mind. Hmmm... "peace of mind". There it is. What I really wanted was peace of mind. I had been depending on him to stop drinking and give it to me, but his drinking choices are not mine to manage. Taking back my peace of mind was mine to manage.

Peace Of Mind

I had been nagging, begging, and pleading for him to stop drinking in order to give me peace of mind. I was stuck on the thought that my peace of mind was dictated by his drinking, because at that space and time, I allowed it to be. But ultimately, my peace of mind was mine to have, with or without the presence of his drinking. I had to shift from dictating the outcome of his desires, and begin to refocus on my desires for peace of mind. This is where ownership for the role you are playing in the codependent; unhealthy relationship begins to take action. I could play the "blame game" all day long for his drinking, but that was not going to solve my angst. I wanted peace of mind.

> *Ego says: 'Once everything falls into place, I'll find peace.'*
>
> *Spirit says: 'Find your peace, and then everything will fall into place.'*
>
> Marianne Williamson

If it brought me peace to spend the whole day out with my family, away from my husband's drinking, that is what I did. I had to let go of the idea that he should be present as my husband to enjoy the family time with my children and I. Letting go of that idea, allowed me to enjoy time with my family, *in peace* without placing demands on his day. Ideally, he would have been a part of a peaceful day; but if he chose otherwise, I had a decision for *peace* or *worry*. I chose peace. If it brought me peace to sit in the car an extra 15 minutes listening to my favorite music before going in the house, that's what I did. If it brought me peace to visit some college friends that I hadn't seen in years, I did it. I was bound and determined to be at peace and I relished in the enjoyment of those moments, as much as possible in order to keep my mind at peace.

Your peace of mind is yours. Be selfish in finding it. I don't encourage being selfish in a spiteful, uncaring way; but selfish in a self-preserving, purposeful way. Prayer, self-exploration,

> " *Your mind and spirit needs healthy fuel to function properly.*"

journaling, creative expression, mindfulness, daily affirmations, and meditation have all been useful in cultivating an internal sense of peace and grounding anxieties. Your mind and spirit needs healthy fuel to function properly.

When your mind is at peace, you are better able to tap into your intuition. As humans, our instincts are present for a reason. They're protective, they're intrinsic, and they adapt based on experience. I'm very intuitive about my feelings and my thoughts, but as you have read, I've been guilty of ignoring them — that's what I call the blindness. Blindness is composed of naiveté and a sense of immaturity that doesn't allow you to truly identify what you feel or communicate it without self-doubt or shame. Therefore, you're prone to go along for the ride against your intuitive judgment and instincts.

Can you truly overcome being a blind passenger?
Or is it something you will always live with?

I believe you can overcome being a blind passenger by being perceptive about your feelings and addressing them accordingly. You may not stop being a passenger based on your love, commitment, or loyalty to someone, but you can remove the blindness and make a clear decision about the relationship. You just need the will to make a decision you can live with. In therapy, my role is to guide people toward a better understanding of their thoughts and feelings, versus remaining in a state of confusion that can hold you emotionally hostage. I encourage people to get educated and validated for the relationship traumas they have experienced because it allows for *clarity, discernment, and decision* in future relationships.

- *Clarity* removes the sticky film and fog from your thoughts, which keeps you in a state of blindness and confusion.

- *Discernment* is the ability to judge well, with purpose and understanding.
- *Decision* is an active and intentional resolution.

> " *With* clarity and discernment, you are able to hold yourself accountable for the role you play in your life situations."

With clarity and discernment, you do not arrive to decisions in your relationship by accident. With clarity and discernment, you are able to hold yourself accountable for the role you play in your life situations. The late Maya Angelou has famously said, "When you know better, do better."

Being on the emotional rollercoaster with your eyes wide open is a totally different experience. You have a renewed vision decide.

In toxic intimate relationships, how do you know whether it's fixable? Whether to stay or not to stay?

As a mental health counselor for individuals, couples, and families, I've been privileged to help people through some pretty treacherous personal situations. Couples in particular are affected by difficulties in the areas of intimacy, fidelity, attachment, abandonment, abuse, and trust. These factors affect the way individuals communicate within the relationship and subsequently how they partner with each other. It's a dance. In the relationship, they are essentially feeding off of each other's energy. As one gives, the other takes; as one withdraws, the other will either withdraw as well or become overbearing/needy in an effort to make up for the lack of interaction. It's a constant tug of war, back and forth, in which one or both of you react in a manner that is detrimental to the relationship, such as—an affair, the silent treatment, the blame game, an old habit, anger outbursts, or perhaps it triggers a mood/anxiety response. In these situations, a third party professional is sought to help sift through some of the murky waters and assist in the healing process to find a resolution.

The magic questions posed to me are "Is this fixable? What's the prognosis? Can we get beyond this? Should we stay together? Am I crazy for feeling this way?" No, you are not crazy; but the prognosis of the relationship depends on the people involved. Each of you need to take responsibility for how your relationship got to the point of discord and the role you play in the tug of war.

I don't play *"blame games"*. Even in situations where one person's behaviors are louder and have a clear detrimental impact, each of you has played a role in the turmoil of the relationship. Instead of pointing the finger at the other, and instead of playing the martyr saying "it's all my fault", I encourage each individual to look in the mirror. What is it about YOU that you're in this situation? What is it about your personality, character, or personal history that has you in this situation? I guarantee we will see some patterns in the way you interact with others throughout your life that contribute to the current difficulties you're having in the relationship. Therefore, whether you decide to stay in the current relationship, break up, separate, or divorce, there is always room for personal improvement and self-reflection that will keep you from repeating some of the same toxic habits. In essence, you are taking those habits and your past relationship issues into the next relationship unless you address it accordingly.

One Last Question...

In telling your story, you will help countless others. When helping them through their situations, how do you stay within yourself? How do you not allow yourself to be triggered by what you may hear?

When I'm working, there are times when self-disclosure is used therapeutically, but I don't get specific about my personal story. Overall, I'm able to validate how they feel, echo their feelings, and allow them to know "I get it". All the while, I aim to keep the focus of the treatment process on them. I'm always moved by the personal stories of others, but it's not my therapy session! Hearing something that reminds me of my personal story, doesn't *"trigger"* me in the sense that I become emotionally affected during the counseling session. It more so raises flags here and there because of the familiarity of emotions expressed by my clients; which is what prompted me to write this book. I've come to recognize that my story is more universal than I initially understood. There are countless others who have, and are going through, similar situations. If I change a few details, people, places, and names, my story easily becomes your story due to the commonality of the emotional experience.

Being a passenger to a loved one's mood swings, addiction, alcoholism, and emotional turmoil allows for a necessary conversation that is often overlooked for the primary identified issue.

With that said, I hope you've found some insight in my experience and will continue to support the conversation. My personal goal in this project is to bring this discussion to the forefront, in an effort to fortify each person's vision to decide.

Epilogue

A self-declared blind passenger in remission, I currently reside in the suburbs of Charlotte, NC with my two daughters. I relocated to the area in 2012 from my hometown in Maryland knowing very few people. As much as I love the comfort and security of my family (the bulk of whom live in Maryland, New Jersey, and New York), I was once again driven by faith and a continuously evolving initiative to be a productive example of responsibility for my two girls. Their mere presence in my life has added weight and urgency to my personal decisions—particularly in my relationships with their fathers—which might have otherwise been prolonged.

Being attached to people with unstable energy is exhausting—emotionally, physically, and at times financially. The roller coaster of their life is furiously intense and it brings a frenzied energy to your life. It is uncomfortable and disappointing to witness and even more infuriating to be a part of. As a ***blind passenger*** and participant on the trip, you have no control. You feel powerless. You're not driving, and often times, neither are they. They are victims of their own self-medicating behaviors and emotional indiscretions, yet they simultaneously permeate stress to the loved ones who are caught up in their path of self-destruction.

As a licensed mental health professional, I have extensive experience working with both mentally ill and drug addicted populations. I have been able to see the depths of many difficult life circumstances and strained relationships. There is usually an identified client with an identified problem, but there are countless *blind passengers* who have been on board for the ride and are vicariously affected along the way. Blinded by love, compassion, ego, embarrassment, and a wealth of other emotions, they are often swept up in the circumstances of the relationship, heavily focused on "*fixing*" their loved one, and unable to get through the tangled mess with their own peace of mind intact.

It has to be nearly impossible to find one person who has not themselves experienced, or had a relationship, that was affected by addiction, domestic violence, emotional instability, or divorce. At this point in our society, these situations are universal to the human experience. So how can we keep denying this conversation? It should no longer be considered a taboo family secret. There is value and purpose in discussing these matters as not to perpetuate the cycle of generational damage and turn a blind eye to a need for personal and familial growth. Through this book, I lead by example.

Being a blind passenger in my marriages was unhealthy for my personal health and emotional sense of security. My energy, spirit, and attitude about life became unsettled while I was entrenched in those relationships. As their primary caregiver, with their well-being in my hands, I was overwhelmed with the responsibility to have a peaceful home. I did not want the toxic environment of alcoholism, drug addiction, emotional instability, and having spiritually divided parents to impact their upbringing in a detrimental fashion. Therefore, tough decisions had to be made.

As a parent, the blind passenger experience has magnified my understanding that my decisions have a direct impact on the development of my children and the type of young women they will grow up to be. Chris Rock tells the classic fatherhood joke of "keeping his daughters off the pole", in reference to loving them enough that they don't end up as strippers seeking the love and attention of other men. Well, I believe it's my job as a mother to create a lifestyle that demonstrates how to choose loving, healthy interactions over those that do not serve your spirit in a positive way. I've learned that I am responsible for the types of relationships I choose to have in my life, and the types of relationships I exemplify to my children. So in essence, I need to lead them to recognize how real love, valuable friendships, and positive interactions look and feel. In turn, this will help them understand that they have a role in being a part of those valuable factors in life.

With both fathers absent from custodial involvement, my biggest challenge as a single parent is being emotionally and physically present. I'm pulled in several directions between the responsibilities of work, home, and two very active children. So I've had to make conscious decisions in my career in order to accommodate a well-rounded life for them. This includes refusing certain job opportunities that might have been higher paying, but also carried higher demands and higher emotional/physical energy—energy that could be spent with and for my children.

In recent years, I transitioned from traditional employment in the mental health field to a self-employed private practice. This allows more flexibility in my work schedule in order to make adjustments for a track meet, a weekly dance practice, or a special school activity. This is what I affectionately call my *"mommy hustle"* as I am constantly trying to manage their schedules with mine. It carries its share of daily stress, but it's the legacy of physical presence and emotional support my parents provided me. I believe it's the foundation for a sense of security and an appreciation for familial bonding that cannot be contrived.

Erin and Imani will always have me as a cheerleader, coach, counselor, comforter, and fan club president on the sideline of their activities. My parents, brother, sister-in-law, God-brother, nephews, and cousins have driven from the DC-Maryland-Virginia area to support them as well. We've also grown a Charlotte-based network of extended family and loved ones in the past 3 years. All of these relationships and the quality of affection and camaraderie they provide are chosen intentionally. The old adage of a *"village"* upbringing is certainly exemplified in our lives with purposeful interactions that foster their social-emotional development. Despite being the product of broken marriage and having a tainted legacy of addiction in their lifelines, I am dedicated to ensure that my girls will never be absent of the concept and feeling of valuable, healthy family relationships.

Artwork by: *Anthony Scruse*

Many hands make light work.
-African Proverb

Acknowledgements

Thank you God for your ever faithful covering!
I've been blessed with a family like no other. I might be
a hollow shell of a woman without a few people at my
backbone:

My parents—Mom and Dad,
Thank you for showing me what a lifetime of respectful
love, friendship, and support looks like in a marriage
and family.

My first playmate, brother, and friend—KJ,
Barbie's and GI Joe's brought us together, but a
balanced recipe of brotherly love, guidance, and
humor has fortified our sibling friendship into our
adulthood and beyond. Thank you for being you.
"You and me, us neva part..."
- Celie and Nettie, The Color Purple

My two loves—Imani and Erin:
You drive me harder than you may ever truly
understand.

Thank you for piercing my blindness and forcing me to be a better woman and mother. Please remember, the boundaries of your heart and mind are controlled by you.

****

To the countless family members, friends, and loved ones I cannot even begin to list—thank you all for keeping me grounded, for giving me something to smile about, and for the occasional glass of wine with a chaser of laughter.

****

I'm so grateful for my fortified faith and daily conversations with God. I know He has guided me through it all. I love my Pastor and Co-Pastor, Shomari and Jacque White, of Have Life Church in Charlotte, NC. Unbeknown to them, their anointing and delivery of the word of God compelled me to sow a seed that I had left dormant. In essence, they empowered me to write this book. It's been an awesome journey. Thank you for building a strong and loving kingdom community.

****

I also want to thank the 3 men discussed in this book for reminding me to fight for my peace of mind. I hope they are able to receive my truth with a healing mindset.

****

And last but not least, to the infinite number of blind passengers in the world—I validate your experience. I pray you find support in the community created from these words. I'm passing the baton of transparency and honesty…I encourage you to continue the necessary conversations.

References

Angelo, Maya. (2015). Page 1
https://www.goodreads.com/author/quotes/
3503.Maya_Angelou

Atsma, Aaron J. (2000). Theoi Project.
http://www.theoi.com/Daimon/Phthonos.ht
ml

Bullfinch's Mythology. (2010). *Phthonus or Phthonos.*
http://levigilant.com/Bulfinch_Mythology/
bulfinch.englishatheist.org/b/pantheon/Pht
honus.htm

Burn, Shawn M. (2013). *Are you in a codependent relationship?* Psychology
Today Blog: Presence of Mind.

Children of Alcoholics. American Association of
Marriage and Family Therapy. (2002).
http://www.aamft.org/iMIS15/AAMFT/Co
ntent/consumer_updates/children_of_alcoh
olics.aspx

Codependency. Mental Health America.
http://www.mentalhealthamerica.net/co-
dependency

Hoffmann, N. G. (2013). Evince Clinical
Assessments
http://www.evinceassessment.com/
UNCOPE_for_web.pdf

Jung, C.G. (1959). *The Archetypes and the
Collective Unconscious*. New York:
Pantheon Books.

Kelly JB & Johnston MP. (2008). Differentiation
Among Types of Intimate Partner
Violence: *Research Update and
Implications for Interventions*. FAMILY
COURT REVIEW, Vol. 46 No. 3, July
2008 476 –499

Konstan, David. (2007). *The Emotions of the
Ancient Greeks: Studies in Aristotle and
Classical Literature* (2007) University of
Toronto Press

Leonard KE. & Eiden RD. (2007). Marital and
Family Processes in the Context of Alcohol
Use and Alcohol Disorder. *Annu Rev of*

Clin Psychol; 3: 285-310. Doi: 1.11466/annurev.clinpsy.3.022806.091424

Mayfield, Curtis., Nelson, Candice C. (2000). Resentment Lyrics. AZLyrics.com http://www.azlyrics.com/lyrics/beyoncekn owles/resentment.html

Merriam-Webster Dictionary. (2015). *Janus-faced.* Merriam-Webster, Incorporated. http://www.merriam-webster.com/dictionary/janus-faced

National Institute on Alcohol Abuse and Alcoholism (NIAAA). (2015). http://www.niaaa.nih.gov/

Phthonos. (2004) Bible Hub. 2011483036 http://biblehub.com/greek/5355.htm

Phthonus. (2013). Wikimedia Foundation, Inc. http://en.wikipedia.org/wiki/Phthonus

Smethers, John E. (2008). *The Prison Stereotype & The Emergence of Puer Aeternus.* SelfGrowth.com http://www.selfgrowth.com/articles/The_Pr ison_Stereotype_the_Emergence_Of_The_ Puer_Aeternus.html (1996 - 2015)

Wilde, Cathy (2013). Heavy drinking is bad for marriage if one spouse drinks, but not both. http://www.buffalo.edu/news/releases/2013/11/031.html

Resources For Assistance

National Alliance on Mental Illness (NAMI)
NAMI Help Line: 1-800-950-NAMI

NAMI, the National Alliance on Mental Illness, is the nation's largest grassroots mental health organization dedicated to building better lives for the millions of Americans affected by mental illness. They provide education, advocacy, and free resources to those with mental illness, as well as the family members.

National Domestic Violence Hotline
1-800-799-SAFE or 1-800-799-7233

National Addiction Hotline
1-866-492-1476

Co-Dependents Anonymous
www.coda.org

Co-Dependents Anonymous is a fellowship of men and women whose common purpose is to develop healthy relationships. The only requirement for membership is a desire for healthy and loving relationships.

Continue The Conversation

MediTate & Mingle is not just a convenient play on my name. It is my personal oxymoron...my yin-yang...my Libra scales...the balancing act that exists within me. *MEDITATE* describes the side of me that is introspective,  cerebral, intuitive, spiritually grounded, and individualized. While the *MINGLE* is my social butterfly, people-person, interactive, talkative side. Bringing them together allows me to reach out to you.

Author Bio

Dr. Tate's knack for writing hit full swing while completing her dissertation for a Doctorate of Education in Counseling Psychology. As a licensed professional counselor with over 10 years of experience working with emotionally disrupted individuals, couples, and families, she has refined a voice for speaking words of wisdom into others and has just recently began to share them with the world in text. In 2014, her writer's blog *MediTate&Mingle* went viral, reaching thousands in the world of social media on the coat tail of her debut article *These Kids Are Getting On My Nerves*. She captures the hearts and funny bones of parents around the world, with a sincere glimpse of an overwhelmed single mom who is seeking a moment's peace from the "little people" who seem to have an ever-growing list of requests (and complaints) amidst an already hectic day. In her book writing debut, Dr. Tate takes the candor to a whole new level. *Blind Passenger* shares some of her personal struggles with damaged family relationships and her fight to regain her peace of mind on an emotional rollercoaster that was driven by mental instability and addictive behaviors. Over the past year, she caught the attention of various radio, news, and television outlets, allowing Dr. Tate a.k.a. Ms. MediTate&Mingle, to extend her mental health know-how to the airways. Hosting her own talk radio show with WGIV Charlotte via internet and TuneIn Radio has provided education and resources about a multitude of topics—bullying, vaccination health, toxic relationships, bipolar disorder, domestic violence, issues of race, socio-political matters, and much more. Dr. Tate pulls from her broad knowledge and experience of working with a vast clientele—some with fairly benign adjustment/phase of life difficulties to the more severe spectrum of suicide, self-harm, psychosis, and trauma. At the heart of it all, she has a passion for breaking down the stigma related to mental health and going to therapy. Dr. Tate maintains a website at www.drmetate.com where you can find additional articles and video clips of her expertise in action.

Need A Speaker

For your event, workshop, conference, etc.....

Contact: BlindPassenger2015@gmail.com

Counselor. Educator. Supervisor. Consultant. Life Coach.

Trainer. Facilitator. Radio Personality. Blogger. Author.

"I enjoy these roles because they position me to pay it forward in a number of ways. My educational background, specialized training, and career experiences allow me to help you continue the necessary conversations."

MediTate&Mingle

is a platform built to jump start conversation about

various mental health topics and social situations that we

all face. We are driven by our thoughts, emotions, impulses,

and instincts in everything we do (or neglect to do).

Relationships, parenting dilemmas, grief/loss, worry,

jealousy, career issues, etc...are all fair topics of discussion.

So join the mental mingle and mediTate with me...

www.drmetate.com

https://twitter.com/drmetate

https://www.facebook.com/Ms.MediTateandMingle

https://www.pinterest.com/msMediTate/